W9-BVK-486

bountiful

RECIPES INSPIRED BY OUR GARDEN

todd porter & diane cu

STEWART, TABORI & CHANG
NEW YORK

Published in 2013 by Stewart, Tabori & Chang
An imprint of ABRAMS

Text copyright © 2013 Todd Porter and Diane Cu
Photographs copyright © 2013 Todd Porter and Diane Cu

All rights reserved. No portion of this book may be reproduced, stored in a retrieval
system, or transmitted in any form or by any means, mechanical, electronic,
photocopying, recording, or otherwise, without written permission from the publisher.

Cataloging-in-Publication Data has been applied for and may be obtained from the
Library of Congress.
ISBN: 978-1-61769-048-8

Editor: Dervla Kelly
Designer: Amy Sly
Production Manager: Tina Cameron

The text of this book was composed in The Serif and Clan.

Printed and bound in Hong Kong, China
10 9 8 7 6 5 4 3 2 1

Stewart, Tabori & Chang books are available at special discounts when purchased
in quantity for premiums and promotions as well as fundraising or educational
use. Special editions can also be created to specification. For details, contact
specialsales@abramsbooks.com or the address below.

THE ART OF BOOKS SINCE 1949
115 West 18th Street
New York, NY 10011
www.abramsbooks.com

To our grandmothers, and all who inspire us to love, cook, and bring together friends and family for raucous good times.

contents

introduction   13

    White on Rice Couple: Our Story   13

    On Sharing   21

    On Cooking and Eating Fresh Produce   22

    On Home Growing   26

garden planning   27

pantry and kitchen notes   32

vegetables   36

tomatoes   39

    Chunky Tomato and Basil Ragu over Polenta   40

    Heirloom Tomato Galettes   43

    Roasted Cherry Tomato and Goat Cheese Dip   45

    Summer Cream of Tomato Soup   48

    Baked Eggs in Tomatoes   51

    Picnic Pasta Salad with Roasted Tomato and Tuna   54

    Zesty Green Tomato Pickles   55

    Homemade Barbecue Sauce from Fresh Tomatoes   56

    Red Tomato Jam with Fresh Ginger   59

herbs & leafy greens   63

    Herbed Garlic Knots   64

    Herb-Crusted Salmon   67

    Basil Pesto Farro Salad   71

    Fresh Herb Pesto   72

    Rosemary Lemonade   74

    Mussels Steamed with Herbs and White Wine   75

    Peppermint Chocolate Chip Ice Cream   79

    Spinach and Bacon Salad with Avocado Vinaigrette   81

    Lettuce Wraps with Almond-Basil Chicken   82

    Creamed Swiss Chard in Goat Cheese on Baked Potatoes   85

    Creamed Dill Chicken Potpie with Puff Pastry   86

beans, stalks & shoots — 89

Creamed Haricots Verts with Toasted Almonds — 90
Tender Roasted Green Beans with Walnuts and Feta — 93
Sautéed Celery and Shrimp — 94
Crispy Soybean Fritters — 97
Quick Pickled Sugar Snap Peas with Mint — 100
Asparagus and Cippolini Quiche — 101
Braised Artichokes in White Wine — 104
Roasted Asparagus Spring Rolls with Bacon — 107
Rhubarb-Vanilla Bread Pudding — 109

broccoli & other cruciferous vegetables — 113

Roasted Broccoli and Grilled Cheese Melt — 114
Spicy Radish Salsa — 116
Braised Brussels Sprouts with Pancetta and Parmesan — 117
Spicy Roasted Cauliflower with Sriracha and Sesame — 118
Grilled Cabbage Wedges — 120
Smashed Cauliflower Sandwiches with Roasted Asparagus — 121
Vietnamese Napa Cabbage Chicken Salad — 124
Warm Kale Salad with Apples and Dried Cranberries — 127
Chopped Kale Salad Massaged with Avocado — 128
Kale and Chicken Egg Rolls with Ginger Soy Dip — 129
Wilted Mizuna Mustard Salad with Shrimp — 131
Arugula with Braised Pork Shoulder — 132

roots & bulbs — 135

Olive Oil-Baked Beet Chips with Sea Salt and Black Pepper — 137
Seared Ginger Carrots with Thyme and Shallots — 138
Roasted Parsley Root with Red Quinoa — 141
Hearty Celery Root and Red Lentil Soup — 142
Potatoes Au Gratin — 145
Herb-Smashed Turnips with Parmesan — 147
Pizza Dough — 148
Pizza with Rosemary Potatoes — 153
Pizza with Caramelized Fennel, Arugula, and Lemon — 154
Jicama Chicken Cashew Salad with Mustard Dressing — 157
Sweet Potato and Chocolate Squares — 158
Sweet Onion Crack Dip — 160

squashes 163

Summer Squash Stuffed with Teriyaki Pork 164

Curried Kabocha Squash and Chicken Stew 167

Roasted Gold Nugget Squash with Apples and Brown Butter 168

Zucchini-Cardamom Mini Tea Cakes 171

Roasted-Pumpkin Ice Cream 172

Roasted Spaghetti Squash with Sausage 175

Butternut Squash Crumble 177

Grilled-Zucchini Banh Mi 178

Roasted and Stuffed Delicata Squash Rings 180

peppers & chilies 183

Charred Bell Peppers and Sausage with Pearled Barley 184

Sweet Pepper and Teriyaki Chicken Skewers 187

Chili Margarita with Paprika Salt 188

Blistered Shishito Peppers with Yuzu Kosho 191

Habanero Chicken Tacos 194

Homemade Sriracha (Chili Hot Sauce) 196

other vegetable fruits 199

Roasted-Corn Tabouli 200

Cucumber Mint Quinoa Salad with Shallot Vinaigrette 203

Miso-Sesame Cucumber Salad 204

Grilled Japanese Eggplants with Orange Zest and Sake Glaze 207

Chunky Roasted Eggplant and Parmesan Dip 208

Corn Fritters 211

Italian-Style Fried Okra 212

Tomatillo Salsa 215

fruit 216

sweet berries 219

Blackberry Cabernet Crisp with Honeyed Whipped Cream 220

Roasted-Strawberry Scones 223

Mixed Berry Chocolate Slab Pie 224

Blueberry Frangipane Tarts 229

Casanova Cocktail 230

Marionberry Mojito Ice Pops 233

citrus 235

Fragrant Orange-Vanilla Muesli 236
Blood Orange Bars with a Brown Butter Crust 237
Meyer Lemon-Iced Brown Butter Madeleines 241
Homemade Orange-Tangerine Soda 243
Classic Bourbon Sour with Orange Bitters 244
Lemon and Cream Spaghetti 247
Tangerine Crème Brûlée 249
Oro Blanco and Watercress Salad 251
Kumquat Marmalade 252
Yuzu Kosho 255

stone fruits 257

Roasted Pluots with Brown Sugar and Balsamic Vinegar 258
Brown Sugar Apricots with Vanilla Rum Ice Cream 261
Vanilla Rum Ice Cream 262
Sautéed Peaches with Brown-Butter Pancakes 263
Stone Fruit Parfait with Orange-Vanilla Granola 266
Peaches with Sabayon and Honey 269
Cherry Bourbon Delight Cocktail 270
Chocolate Cherry Crisp 273

other tree & vine fruits 275

Butterscotch-Apple Mini Galettes 276
Grape, Arugula, and Brie Bruschetta 279
Fig and Gorgonzola Pillows 281
Puff Pastry Dough 284
Pear-Dorf Salad 287
Gin Cocktail with Pomegranate and Grapefruit 288
Fresh Persimmon Cookies with Raisins and Nuts 291
Homemade Pineapple Teriyaki Sauce 292
Honeydew Salad with Riesling and Mint 293
Fresh Cantaloupe Jam 294
Watermelon Mojito 297
Melon Sangria 298

index 300
acknowledgments 304

"If you really want to make a friend, go to someone's house . . . the people who give you their food give you their heart."

—Cesar Chavez

white on rice couple: our story

A GIRL FROM VIETNAM

With my first bite into an American cheeseburger, I was smitten. Though I was only about four years old, this food moment is still vivid for me. The taste of that thin, floppy burger was so different from my regular regimen of rice and noodles. And the pickle—oh, that soggy, briny thing was just wonderful; I had always had an addiction to anything sour, so that pickle laced with tart mustard and sweet ketchup was like candy. Then there was the cheese: That melted-yellow creaminess on top of the meat was super-decadent and satisfying. My cheeks swelled with delight and my belly was instantly in love.

Beyond just the burger, that meal ignited an awareness of the world of food beyond my mother's everyday kitchen fare of white rice, fresh vegetables, fish, pho noodles, and more fish.

Vietnamese food was what I was born into. The pulse and heartbeat of what resonates in my soul and fills my pantry are the flavors defined by growing up Vietnamese: spicy, salty, sour, sweet, and savory—with plenty of liquid-gold fish sauce.

I was born in Da-Nang in 1972, and my childhood world was consumed by stories of the Vietnamese war: of conflict, of suffering, of loss, and of how little food there was to eat. I was taught to eat everything off my plate, because every grain of white rice was made out of love and sacrifice.

Again and again, every conversation and bit of wisdom ended up with a lesson in food. Whether it was a reminder that people are starving in the world or a pointer on how I could have pounded the lemongrass finer, I was schooled through food.

I'm grateful for those reminders now, as an adult. Ask me how grateful I was back then, as a third-grader, and I'd probably tell you that all I wanted for dinner was a pepperoni pizza. ("Oh, why not? Rice *again*?") But now I'm so grateful for everything my parents have given me that it almost hurts.

In 1975, when I was two-and-a-half years old and Mom was three months pregnant with my brother, we fled Da-Nang along with my uncle and paternal grandmother. Like so many other Vietnamese families during that treacherous time, we fled, ran for our lives, hid, then made it onto a boat: a very big boat packed tight with frightened people. We floated on the open ocean, without fresh water and with scarcely any food; babies screamed, adults cried, and lives were lost. We eventually ended up in a refugee camp in Guam. My father was in the South Vietnamese navy and fought alongside the American forces. He was separated from us during our escape, but thankfully we were all reunited at that refugee camp.

That's how I remember describing the experience to my schoolteachers in third grade. My English vocabulary was very limited back then, but that's pretty much how I shared the story. I often like to draw back on my third-grade jabber because, quite frankly, it's less graphic and painful than what really went on. The rawer, more truthful memories I inherited from Mom are only for times when I have a bottle of bourbon by my side.

After a few months in the refugee camp, we came to America and went to live with my aunt, who was married to an American soldier and already living in the States. Since 1975, my parents have relieved me of my only-child status by adding five more siblings to my big-sister résumé. Growing up in a family of six kids meant having to share, explore, study, sleep, drink, and sometimes even shower as a group. But most important of all, it meant cooking and eating together.

Mom and Dad were infatuated with food, and they now had six kids in their arsenal of free labor for growing, cooking, and executing their crazy food parties. We were always asked to participate in household cooking chores (or, in our eyes, torture-pain-suffering), and no video games were permitted until we were finished. As a fourth-grader, I was not happy.

Actually, my parents were more than infatuated; they were possessed. They tore up the backyard patch of green grass to grow a mini vegetable farm. With the help of six kids, they were able to grow and harvest fresh vegetables, lush Asian greens, and loads of fresh herbs. Each child was born into the role of a line-cook. I helmed lemongrass pounding at the mortar and pestle and manned the shrimp-peeling station. My younger siblings fulfilled their respective roles as garlic masher, shallot peeler, herb washer, eggplant picker, and lime squeezer with civic duty.

I had a love-hate relationship with food when I was growing up because preparing it was always so complicated and time consuming. Food had to be fresh, because that's the only way my parents knew how to feed us. If we were hungry, we had to grow the food, pick it, wash it, then cook it. It was beyond my understanding that some of my American friends had it as easy as buying dinner at a fast-food restaurant or cooking a ready-made boxed meal. I was seething with jealousy every time I had to prep for my parents' fried-fish dinners.

My love of heavy cheese dishes, fried chicken, burgers, pizza, Twinkies, and other junk food drove me to distraction when I had to eat rice, noodles, and fresh herbs and greens, again and again. I just wanted to have a soft, chewy chocolate chip cookie! My hunger was certainly satisfied by Vietnamese food and I was fulfilled with a bowl of noodles, but eating a burger or pizza meant that I was more American.

It wasn't until I moved away from home to the small town of Port Angeles, Washington, at the age of twenty-two and as a vegetarian, that I learned the value of the cooking I had been raised on. Living far away from my parents' kitchen meant that I was able to eat all the cheese pizza and potato chips I wanted. At first, it was a blessing not to have to peel and devein shrimp and be free from the throngs of the home kitchen.

Food had to be fresh because that's the only way my parents knew how to feed us. If we were hungry, we had to grow the food, pick it, wash it, then cook it.

It wasn't until I began breaking down both physically and spiritually that I realized I was yearning for a home-cooked meal. I needed Vietnamese food and I needed it fast and plentiful. (I found myself craving the flavor of fresh mint—what a crazy thought that was back then, to actually wish I had an herb to gnaw on!) I was malnourished and puffed out from eating bags of bagels and cream cheese. I had to learn how to cook for and feed myself the best way that I knew how.

All of a sudden, I was searching for ways to prepare vegetables even remotely close to how Mom would have done or to make the soup that Dad would simmer for hours. Drawing back on every oral recipe Mom had taught me, on every kitchen technique Dad had drilled into my head, and on every memory of what had stocked their kitchen, I taught myself how to cook fresh food.

I traveled for hours sourcing ingredients that were not readily available to me in the small town where I lived. I relished farmer's markets because the vegetables there looked like what came out of my parents' garden. I liberated myself from the mounds of junk food and was now swimming in fresh greens, garlic, shallots, and vegetables again. I even owned my own knife, stockpot, cast-iron pan, and mortar and pestle, all tools that are bound to my heart and will go with me to my grave.

Home cooking was emerging from my tiny kitchen far away from home. I was humbled beyond measure—and grateful for every single cooking lesson, verbal recipe, grain of rice, and pearl of food wisdom that ever crossed my plate and my path.

And as for that cliché that we eventually become our parents? In my case, it's completely true. Look at my backyard today and I'm living proof of life's ironies, contradictions, and homecomings. My journey with food becomes more challenging and more exciting every day. I'm so grateful to everyone who nursed me through this delicious life that it hurts—but in a beautiful way.

A BOY FROM A CATTLE RANCH IN OREGON

It's hard to say when my love of food began. It feels as if there was no beginning, as if it was always there.

I grew up on a cattle ranch in northeastern Oregon, a land of valleys nestled into the mountains, dotted with small towns centered around farming and logging. In the summer you can climb the foothills and look out across the patchwork quilt of crops filling the valleys, with a lazy river meandering through and breaking up the perfect squares of farmland.

From the time I was knee-high, my memories were filled with the scents of hay and horses, the feel of newborn calves sucking on fingers with their rough tongues and budding teeth. Even today, more than thirty years later, I can vividly recall the sights and sounds of feeding milk formula to orphaned calves we'd pasture next to the house, their cold, wet noses poking through the fences as they stretched to reach the bottles they would then fiercely suck on.

My youth was filled with adventures of tramping through waist-high pastures, grasshoppers scattering with every stride; of fishing for trout and searching for crawdads in the creek that wound through our property and lent its name to our ranch.

The Indian Creek Ranch. A small ranch focused on raising Hereford cattle, and now a place that no longer exists as I knew it, lost to the changing of industries and lives. It is, however, a place that shall forever be ingrained in my heart. It was life on that ranch, combined with the ever-present love and encouragement of my parents, that laid the foundation for the person I am today.

You see, life on a ranch can be quite isolated and quiet. Our nearest neighbor was about half a mile away, and to get to the nearest family with kids our age we'd have to tack on another couple of miles. Days were punctuated with chores and responsibilities, with the long gaps in between filled with exploration and imagination.

When confronted with a problem, or boredom, there was no one outside yourself to help alleviate it. If the pipes froze over in the horses' water trough, as a young kid you'd just figure out how to thaw the pipes and fix the problem. When the cattle or horses broke out, whoever was home would round them up, find the downed fence, and repair it. The thought of us being "just kids" never came into the equation. There were no limits to what we could do, except those we placed on ourselves.

There were so many things when I was growing up that seemed so commonplace at the time; only after much time and distance away from them did I realize how special they were. We grew up drinking the milk from a few milking cows we had pastured near the barn. The rich milk would be placed in the fridge, letting the cream rise to the top so it could be easily skimmed off. It took me forever to get used to the milk served in our elementary

school. Those first experiences drinking milk from a carton made me think I was drinking milklike water.

There were some things that were special, even to us as kids. Homegrown raspberries had to be the greatest things ever. The horses thought so too, and we had to double up the fence just to keep them from stretching their mouths across and devouring every berry within reach. But we would make it up to them by bringing armfuls of apples from the front-yard trees. Oh that sweet aroma under those trees! Just the thought takes me back, and to the remembrance of dodging the bees attracted to the same beautiful scents.

Although no one else in the house was obsessed with cooking, there was one grandma in particular who etched into me her love for it. Even though we saw only her a handful of times as we were growing up, each of those visits left me with lasting food memories. It was she who left me with my first memory of cooking, and of trying octopus, and of learning as a five-year-old that I actually liked cooked carrots. Just like many kids I thought I hated them, until she affectionately but unwaveringly insisted I try them. "You don't have to eat them all, just try them."

Throughout my life those etchings from the ranch have guided me. In the isolation of ranch life, I had learned to listen to my instincts.

As I grew older, I found myself drawn more and more into the kitchen. We all had varying schedules, and there was always a freezer full of meat, so in my early teens I started cooking for myself. Cookbooks and magazines were my guides as I experimented and learned. I was also lucky enough to have parents who supported nearly everything my sister and I did. (I once filled the house with the fumes of a particularly vinegary orange sauce, and there was no word of complaint or protest.)

In my later teens, I discovered cooking a meal for a girl was a great way to get a date, especially in a sleepy little town where there was not much else to do. And after that there was no looking back. I studied Italian cooking, Asian cuisine, sauces, pastries, breads—anything I could find a cookbook about or a magazine to inspire me with. In the kitchen, time disappeared, and the world of food became a beautiful beacon leading me forward.

Throughout my life those etchings from the ranch have guided me. In the isolation of ranch life, I had learned to listen to my instincts. I became self-sufficient, often self-taught, and always open to exploration and discovery.

After high school it was time for a change. I left behind the mountains, valleys, streams, and horses for a vastly different life. I loaded all I could onto my motorcycle and rode over a thousand miles south to attend college in Southern California. Several years into college, after spending a couple of years working part time in coffeehouses and restaurants, I decided my major was far less interesting than the culture of food. *That* was where my heart was.

It wasn't long before I met the love of my life, and things have never been the same since. She was a veg-head from the rice paddies of Vietnam and I was a boy from a cattle ranch in the foothills of Oregon, but bound by our love of food, exploration, and each other, we were a perfect match.

Today, even though I'm far removed from the life of the cattle ranch and the quiet of the countryside, the spirit of the boy who jumped from rock to rock to cross a creek, spent afternoons chasing herds of deer on horseback, and found ways to lug bales of hay heavier than himself still resides within me. There is a part of me who is still a boy cooking for his girl, receiving untold joy from seeing her face light up after she's enjoyed something I've made. After all, how can a girl resist a boy who bakes?

TOGETHER AS WHITE ON RICE COUPLE

The initial seeds were planted in 1996, when we had our first conversations about food together. Over warm mochas in a coffeehouse, we bonded over subjects like art, theatre, love of the great outdoors, gardening, and, of course, food.

Back then, while the rest of our peers were hitting the nightclubs, we were at home watering our herb pots and learning how to make puff pastry. We're a little embarrassed to admit that at the time we were full-fledged food nerds, with a little garden geek thrown in. Yes, we were the homebodies who would rather stay home on a Saturday night and bake bread while the rest of our friends did what most young people did—which was *not* to stay at home and hover over the stove.

Even in our first two years in a small second-story apartment, we managed to start our first garden with potted vegetable plants packed onto a tiny balcony. Although it was limiting, we were determined to begin growing herbs and small fruit trees. From this special gathering place, growing, feeding, sharing, and cooking inspiration flowed.

Over the next decade we continued to build our food life in our small kitchens. We both worked long hours at day jobs that rarely allowed us to see each other. Todd worked in restaurant management, and Diane photographed families in her portrait studio. We'd both work long days, then meet back up at home to cook together while discussing how we could develop a life of working together rather than apart.

After a few failed attempts to find a location where we could open a restaurant together, we realized this was an omen. Instead of pursuing the restaurant plan to satisfy our love of food and cooking, we took a different route through photography, but we still wanted to be connected to the food community in some way.

While browsing online one day, we came across websites on which people were sharing their experiences about food. These "food blogs" were full of personal recipes, photographs,

food stories, restaurant reviews, and everything that had to do with food. Reading these blogs inspired us to join this incredibly connected community of food people. We knew we wanted to be a part of it, even if just to share our garden stories and recipes.

From there, we whimsically came up with the name "White On Rice Couple." Why this name? Because we wanted to poke fun at our ourselves and our cultural differences. Also, this name was available for only ten dollars a year, which seemed like a minimal investment for a personal hobby.

Thus, in 2008, WhiteOnRiceCouple.com was born. It has since evolved into a life-changing experience that we never expected. Our stories and photographs about our personal recipes, our garden triumphs and failures, our families, our dogs, and pretty much everything we wanted to share about our lives poured into each post. If something died in the garden, we wrote about it. When we had a bumper crop of vegetables and made a fun soup from them, it was certain to make the Monday blog post.

Never in our wildest dreams did we imagine that this silly-named blog would be interesting to people, let alone lead us to a creative new career in food photography, food styling, filmmaking, and recipe writing. Now our days are filled with styling, photographing, and producing visual multimedia video, films, and other content for national brands, publishers, magazines, and newspapers. Traveling the world to teach workshops, speak at conferences, and meet our food community face to face is what drives us to pursue this life of worldwide communication.

Thanks to the support, encouragement, comments, and friendship of everyone within the food blogging community, we have found the inspiration to continue sharing and doing what we love so much to do.

on sharing

Everything about growing and cooking food brings us comfort. To be able to make things with our hands is satisfying, but to be able to share it with others is the ultimate joy and privilege. We're grateful to have others at our table alongside us, with whom to break bread, to tell stories, and to cultivate friendship through eating and sharing.

Food is powerful that way.

The food we make and eat is about community, nurturing, and letting others know that we care and that they are loved. In the very beginning of our life as a couple, we didn't have much in the way of money or material belongings. But what we always had was a meal, a platter of cookies, or a pie to share. And we always accepted the same with open arms when someone gave to us something they had made with their own hands.

Feeding one another is undeniably a loving way to connect.

We are often asked what makes our cooking different, what makes food such an integral part of our lives, and what makes our garden grow. For us, it's not about what food means to us or what gets us cooking, but rather *why* we cook. We cook because it nurtures us in more ways than we can ever imagine. Without food and cooking, our souls would be empty and lifeless. This process—from growing and harvesting to cooking and feeding—fuels our love for one another and our appreciation for life on its simplest terms.

Gathering at the table is the culmination of everything we believe in. Our table will always be full with stories and friendship, even if what we eat is a mere loaf of bread. Our sincerest hope is that you take time to sit, eat, and share together. Life's most powerful moments happen at the table.

Food brings people together in magical ways.

on cooking & eating fresh produce

With the changing of the seasons, our little patio garden reminded us of what to anticipate for the next meal. Meals began to be focused around fresh produce. This was not optional; it was a necessity integral to our lifestyle. In fact, there was no way to avoid fresh fruits and vegetables in the way we lived and worked.

Being able to grow seasonal fruits and vegetables as part of our daily lives all year round reminds us to eat mindfully and healthfully. Because of this access to produce in our garden and amazing finds in local markets, our meals have always been focused around fresh fruit and vegetables. Although we do eat meat, our recipes often highlight produce as the hero of the dish.

Way back in 1996, when Diane was a vegetarian and Todd worked in a vegetarian restaurant, our daily meals included vegetables in every possible preparation. Entrees and appetizers always showcased fresh produce. Between our long Southern California growing seasons and the numerous local farmer's markets, we were never without a satisfying vegetable.

Our budget was tight too, as we had very little between us while we were working to build our life together. Expensive items like meats and cheese were a luxury. And the times when Todd would splurge a little to buy a nice cut of meat were few and far between. What we could always afford to grow or buy were fruits and vegetables. Anything that was green, leafy, or fruity we were able to make into a meal. Our obsession with produce grew with abandon; without it our cooking would feel strange and incomplete.

Over the years, we concentrated our creative energy on making fresh seasonal produce as distinctive and gratifying as possible on the plate. If we had a squash, we'd experiment with different preparations—using spices, fresh herbs, and soy sauce—to make it into a tasty and substantial meal. There is never a dull moment with fruit and vegetables. In your cooking, consider how to make use of the extra vegetables in your refrigerator. Even forgotten greens hiding in the vegetable drawer can transform into something wonderful.

Although we now both eat meat regularly, we'll often prepare a dinner and realize that it is completely vegetarian. Produce has become such a star in our dishes that we rarely miss meat when there is none in a meal. If you have veggie-haters in your family, however, try introducing them to a vegetable or fruit in a way that they've never had before. Summer squash, for example, is versatile, both as a salad and as a main dish on the barbecue. Grilled zucchini burgers topped with homemade fresh-tomato sauce will be a surprise hit at your next cookout—don't tell anyone that there's no meat in them because they probably won't even notice! Consider these recipes as a clever way to sneak in vegetables without picky eaters knowing it. You'll be feeding your family healthy food without force, and you can naturally build up to making fresh foods the heroes of your meals.

We're hoping this book will provide you with many options for when your CSA box is brimming with exciting produce. When the stalls at your farmer's market are at their peak, or when your garden graces you with a handful of tomatoes, you'll find a recipe in this cookbook to make a complete seasonal meal. On the other hand, if you live in a region with a short growing season and limited farmer's markets, but have access to grocery stores with quality year-round produce, there are recipes here that feature even common vegetables such as celery, radishes, eggplant, and potatoes. We don't always have access to seasonal foods, and making use of easy-to-find but healthy options is important.

We've tried our best to make sure that no matter where you live, what your income status is, and what your eating habits are, there is a fruit or vegetable waiting for you to fall in love with in this cookbook.

Have fun, and enjoy nature's bounty.

on home-growing

Our kitchen is the heart of our home but the garden is its soul. The garden has not only nourished us; it has also given us wisdom, sanctuary, and inspiration. We've learned more through failures in gardening than from anything else we've put our hands to.

We started off as a couple of kids who wanted to grow stuff we liked to eat; our gardens haven't been built with the experience and knowledge of master gardeners. The couple with whom we shared our first apartment graciously let us take over its tiny patio, and it wasn't long before we had it overflowing with potted plants—overflowing, at least, when we weren't exercising our brown thumbs and letting sections of the plants dry up and die.

Through trial and error we slowly started finding our way. Ironically, the more plants we began to grow, the less effort it was. Fresh herbs were continually being used in the kitchen, and the more we cooked with them, the less we would forget about taking care of the plants on the patio. We became more consistent in watering and fertilizing them. The herbs would get regularly pinched back, fostering fresh new growth. It wasn't long before we were trying to grow dwarf citrus trees on that tiny patio. Our first tree is still growing, now in the ground in our current garden, nearly seventeen years later.

Not everyone has a backyard in which to grow fruits and vegetables. Don't feel as if you need a plot of land to garden. Remember, we started our garden on a tiny apartment balcony with pots, which sparked our love of growing.

Small potted herbs are a wonderful kickoff for first time gardeners like we were. For those of you who live in tiny apartments, with just a sunny windowsill, consider growing a few of your favorite herbs in pots. Being able to harvest sprigs of fresh basil or thyme from your windowsill garden is truly gratifying.

The joy of growing isn't about who has the biggest garden. For us, the love of growing lies in the quality of plants and how happy a small sprig of fresh mint can make us feel.

garden planning

With enough land to play with, we finally stumbled upon one of the most successful elements of a good garden: planning. There was so much we wanted to grow, but in order to make the most of our space, we needed to plan it out. And our first step was to create a design for our garden. Our process is just one of many ways to begin a garden, but it has helped us create a place where people, plants, and nature settle in harmony.

- Draw inspiration from magazines, funky or boutique nurseries, botanical gardens, and other people's homes; start mapping out how to develop the garden.

- Study how the sun falls on the garden throughout the day.

- Envision gatherings in the garden; plan for little nooks and seating areas where people can gather and have conversations.

- Create different places to relax in the garden throughout the day, some where the morning light is beautiful, others for the afternoon. Imagine little places to get lost in and explore.

After we spent months clearing out weeds, trimming overgrown plants, and doing other chores to wipe our garden's canvas clean, these are some of the basics we built our garden's structure on:

Begin with the "bones" of the garden. Start by planning pathways, trees, planters, and other elements that will be hard to change after they are in place. (Don't underestimate how big some trees can get. They may look cute in the nursery, but they can quickly grow into something you'll be struggling to keep trimmed down year after year.) The "bones" will determine the flow through your garden. Pathways dictate the movement patterns. Trees control the shade and influence the airflow. Arches and trellises allow plants to act as doorways and walls, giving just a glimpse of what lies beyond.

Seek out help from your local experts. One of the biggest mistakes we made in the beginning was not asking for guidance from the local nurseries and gardeners. It eased our learning curve tremendously once we started talking to people with practical knowledge about growing plants in our region.

Beyond the local nurseries, make inquiries at gardening clubs, explore online gardening forums, and chat it up with other green-thumbed souls. The advice from these people is invaluable. Shared wisdom can help you listen to your plants more closely and become a better gardener.

Plan your water system. Anything you'll need to dig and lay pipe or tubing for should be installed early in the design and building stage. This may be just adding a faucet or two for easier access, or it could involve several drip irrigation systems set on timers to automate and control the watering. We are lucky to live in a region where our drip irrigation system can stay out all year, but in colder areas you'll need to drain and bring in the tubing during the winter. If you have to add a water system after the garden is already established, it can still usually be done, but it may not be nearly as convenient or as pretty to build.

Make a list of plants you want to grow. These can include whatever your senses fall in love with—colors you find beautiful, or scents and textures you love. Also plan to grow crops you love to eat—things you can't find in the local markets or that are expensive to buy.

Find out which plants grow well in your region. Visit local nurseries and gardens for new inspiration and unique plant finds. Sometimes you'll stumble upon a native plant you fall in love with, or you can save yourself heartache by discovering that a plant you love just won't do well where you live. (Don't forget to ask the other customers too. We all have our favorites, and many garden geeks roving the aisles love to talk about them!)

Research the appearance of plants and trees throughout the entire year. This can save you from disappointing plantings. A deciduous tree is a great choice to shelter the house or shade a seating area during the hot summer, then allow the sun to come through to warm that same area when it loses its leaves in the winter. On the other hand, a plant may dazzle you during its one-month flowering stage, but then you could end up with a look you don't really like for the remaining eleven months. Make sure you'll enjoy the plants not just in their prime, but in their least attractive state as well.

Create a beautiful, practical, and edible garden. If you're going to plant a tree, why not a tree that could provide something edible to enjoy, or at least attract beneficials such as local birds? Many herbs are edible and also make fantastic ground covers. (Just be careful of some; mint can quickly get out of control if not contained.)

Choose plant locations based on their need for sunlight. Acquaint yourself with the sunlight needs of plants in your area and plant accordingly. A trellised section might block the sun from other plants needing that warmth, but when reversed in position both may grow well. Even though many herbs are listed as needing full sun, in areas with harsher summers they may do better with a gentle filtered sun. We tuck ours in pots under the shade of our fruit trees, and they stay more tender during the hotter months.

Build raised vegetable planters. They can be filled with soft, fluffy soil that won't get compressed by foot traffic. Our dogs hardly ever set foot in them, choosing to cruise the pathways instead. When you build raised planters, wider rows tend to be much more effective than narrow ones, giving the roots room to stretch and allowing a greater diversity in planting.

Allow an ecosystem to develop. This way the garden will work for you instead of against you. If you create the opportunity for beneficial bugs and predators to your pests to thrive, you'll spend less time fighting the troublemakers. Don't immediately try to wipe out every bug in the garden. Find bugs that will do the work for you.

Mulch, mulch, mulch. The weed's worst enemy—and your best friend for water retention—is mulch. You don't always need to buy it in bags either. Hedge trimmings and other leaves often make great mulch.

Gardens take time and care and are never done; they continue to evolve as our needs and desires change. They can be a source of great pleasure or, if not planned to suit your lifestyle, they can be a great burden. Taking the time to plan your garden will help determine which way it affects you.

We began with our herbs and trees, planned well, and built up from there. At first there were a lot of hours put in after work and on days off: cleaning out weeds and overgrowth, digging and laying pathways, building planters, and amending soil. Today, however, all of that planning and work have paid off, and it seems like the garden almost takes care of itself.

Throughout the year, the garden is always offering new surprises and delights. We are constantly learning from it and it influences our lives tremendously. We appreciate the seasons and the rhythm of nature more. We watch others delight in how amazing a fresh-picked fruit can taste. It teaches us patience. It inspires and brings ease to fresh, amazing cooking. There is no more running out to the store to get parsley or lemon; we just patter out into the garden.

For us, any time and effort put into the garden is repaid a hundred times over. Picking a gently sun-warmed, sugary-sweet tangerine from the tree. Watching the butterflies and hummingbirds flit about the garden. Seeing our friends instantly unwind and become giddy when they see a favorite fruit growing or discover something new. When people walk through our front gate, it is like entering another world. And it happens to be a particularly delicious one.

pantry & kitchen notes

Subtleties and variances in ingredients can lead to success or failure when you are making a recipe. Here are a few key elements to help you have the most success with our recipes in your kitchen.

INGREDIENTS

EGGS Unless otherwise noted, egg size is large. We encourage you to find free-range eggs whenever possible. Not only do they taste better, but you'll also be supporting someone trying to make a little difference in the world.

SUGAR Unless otherwise noted, "sugar" means granulated sugar. "Brown sugar" refers to golden brown sugar (also sold as light brown sugar). "Confectioners' sugar" is also sold as powdered sugar or icing sugar.

SALT We used Morton Coarse Kosher Salt in all our recipes, for consistency in taste and measurement. Every salt will have a different impact on taste in a recipe, mostly due to variance in crystal size. We prefer a flaky salt to a finer-grained table salt in cooking. It allows a more layered taste on the palate rather than a uniform saltiness, allowing each flavor to shine a little more distinctly. That doesn't mean you have to use Morton Coarse Kosher Salt every time you cook—when cooking for ourselves, we will often use a sea salt found in a local market—but knowing how salt in our recipes is measured will give you a starting point for your salting. In general, if you are using table salt, use less than our recipes call for. If you are using Diamond Crystal Kosher Salt, use more. If you are using a sea salt, try to find out which crystal it most closely resembles and base your adjustments on that.

- About ¾ tablespoon table salt = 1 tablespoon Morton Coarse Kosher Salt
- 1 tablespoon Morton Coarse Kosher Salt = 1½ tablespoons Diamond Crystal Kosher Salt

FLOUR Unless otherwise noted, "flour" means unbleached all-purpose flour. An important note, especially for pastries: Different brands of flour can vary greatly in their volume-to-weight ratio, and the way you fill the measuring cup will also affect density. For the best results, we highly recommended measuring flour by weight instead of volume.

vegetables

TOMATOES • HERBS & LEAFY GREENS •
BEANS, STALKS & SHOOTS • BROCCOLI & OTHER CRUCIFEROUS
VEGETABLES • ROOTS & BULBS • SQUASHES •
PEPPERS & CHILIES • OTHER VEGETABLE FRUITS

tomatoes

FROM OUR FIRST BITE INTO A JUICY HEIR-loom tomato at the farmer's market, we were hooked—you might even say obsessed, when you consider how we attempt to duplicate the same bounty in our backyard. Luscious, vibrant tomatoes in all different colors, sizes, and flavors stud our garden all season long.

In our current garden space, we're maxed out with about twenty heirloom tomato plants. Every spring it's difficult to select which new varieties we want to try and which ones we must repeat from the previous seasons. It's almost impossible, like making a mother choose her favorite child. All of our tomato plants are our babies, each with its individual character and personality.

Southern California weather is kind to our tomato garden, and we're spoiled by warm springs and summers in which to nurture the vines and fruit. But growing tomatoes in a coastal climate isn't without its challenges. Pests, bugs, and mildew have ruined many of our growing seasons. Patience, research on our growing zone, and careful attention to the plants have finally taught us how to grow tomatoes successfully. Rotating crops and taking care of the soil have been key. Neem oil has been a godsend in our battles with mildew.

Our list of favorite heirloom tomato varieties is long, plentiful, and always changing: Black Cherokees, Kentucky Beefsteaks, Sungolds, Sweet Millions, all the different Zebra varieties, and Anna Russians are just a few on our current tomato-love-affair list. The cherry tomato varieties in particular are a regular indulgence in the summer, like perfectly sweet garden candy. When they are warmed by the morning sun, we find ourselves wandering the garden and picking them by the handful to snack on.

Salads, sauces, soups, jams, preserves, and other tomato dishes churn out of our kitchen all summer long. It's never tiring to cook with tomatoes; the creative possibilities are endless. For those young, green tomatoes that never make it to fruition, we also have pickles, chutneys, and frying recipes to fall back on, so no tomato goes to waste.

Treat yourself to a swipe of goat cheese on fried bread, topped with a thick slice of heirloom tomato and slivers of fragrant basil. You'll see why one of our freshest and simplest meals can be so addictive. It's that easy to fall in love with a great, humble tomato.

chunky tomato and basil ragu over polenta

SERVES 2 TO 3

Polenta has so much potential in the kitchen, and our dear friend, author and TV chef Cristina Ferrare helped us embrace the endless possibilities of this versatile grain. Here, we paired a slow ragu of tomatoes with gently fried polenta disks. When the chill of autumn starts to arrive and you can still get your hands on a late-summer batch of tomatoes, this hearty dish is perfect to fuel the soul.

INGREDIENTS

2 tablespoons unsalted butter

½ medium onion, chopped (about ½ cup / 80g)

1 pound (455g) ripe tomatoes, chopped

¼ teaspoon kosher or sea salt

Freshly cracked black pepper

2 tablespoons olive oil

1 (1-pound / 455-g) tube polenta, sliced ½ inch (12 mm) thick

1 bunch fresh basil, chopped

½ cup (50g) freshly grated Parmesan

DIRECTIONS

1 In a large pan, melt the butter over medium-low heat. Add the onion and cook until soft.

2 Add the tomatoes, salt, and pepper. Reduce the heat to low and simmer for about 30 minutes. Set aside.

3 In a large skillet, heat the oil over medium heat. Fry each side of the polenta disks just until warm and soft. Do not fry the polenta too much or it will become mushy and break apart.

4 Serve the tomato ragu over the polenta disks and garnish with the basil and Parmesan.

heirloom tomato galettes

MAKES 2 (8-INCH / 20-CM) GALETTES

One of our favorite ways to use pastry is to make a galette. Beautiful and rustic, it wraps its edges around the filling but still leaves the center open to spotlight what lies within: gorgeous, fleshy tomatoes like Kentucky Beefsteaks and Brandywines. The Parmesan–cream cheese base here adds a touch of richness to contrast with the sweet tomatoes. (Pesto, such as the Fresh Herb Pesto on page 72, makes a great alternative base filling.)

INGREDIENTS

FOR THE FILLING

2 ounces (57g) freshly grated Parmesan

2 ounces (57g) cream cheese, at room temperature

¼ cup (60g) mayonnaise

¼ medium onion, diced (about ¼ cup / 40g)

1 teaspoon fresh thyme leaves

Freshly cracked black pepper

FOR THE CRUST

2 cups (250g) flour

½ cup (1 stick / 113g) cold unsalted butter, cut into ½-inch (12-mm) pieces

1 teaspoon kosher or sea salt

1 egg

¼ cup (60ml) cold water

Heavy cream, for brushing crust

3 to 4 medium tomatoes, sliced ¼ inch (6 mm) thick

DIRECTIONS

1 Preheat the oven to 375°F (190°C). Line two sheet pans with parchment paper.

2 **Make the filling:** In a bowl, mix the Parmesan, cream cheese, mayonnaise, onion, thyme, and pepper to taste until well combined. Set aside.

3 **Make the crust:** In a separate bowl, pinch together the flour, butter, and salt with your fingertips until most of the big chunks of butter are flattened or broken up.

4 In a third bowl, whisk the egg with the ice water until combined. Incorporate the egg mixture into the flour until the mixture binds together and forms a rough ball (you may need to gently knead the ball to incorporate the last of the flour).

5 Divide the ball in two, roll each half into a ball, and then flatten each ball into a disk.

6 Wrap one disk in plastic wrap and place it in the fridge. On a floured surface, roll the other disk out to a circle slightly larger than 10 inches (25-cm) in diameter.

7 Trim the dough into an even 10-inch (25-cm) circle (we use a 10-inch / 25-cm ring mold to cut the dough). Gently wrap the dough around a rolling pin, then unroll it onto one of the prepared sheet pans. Repeat with the other dough ball.

recipe continues

8 Spoon half of the Parmesan–cream cheese mixture in the center of one dough circle, spreading the mixture out evenly to within about 2 inches (5 cm) of the outside edge.

9 Place one to two layers of sliced tomatoes over the cheese mixture.

10 Fold the edge of the dough over the tomatoes. Brush the crust with the cream.

11 Repeat the filling, folding, and brushing procedure with the second dough circle and the remaining ingredients.

12 Bake for 50 to 60 minutes, or until the crust is golden, rotating the pans halfway through so the galettes will bake evenly.

13 Serve warm or at room temperature.

roasted cherry tomato and goat cheese dip

SERVES 4 TO 6

A few of our favorite varieties of cherry tomatoes to grow are heirloom Sungolds, Sweet Million, and Black Cherry. At the peak of summer, cherry tomatoes are nature's candy, and to munch on a handful of them and appreciate their pops of natural sugar is a simple treat. But it can be hard to keep up with them when they all explode on the vines at once. Roasting them with some goat cheese in a great savory dip to spread on crackers is a terrific way to manage surplus cherry bombs and highlight fresh cherry tomatoes as appetizers.

INGREDIENTS

3 tablespoons olive oil

½ pound (225g) cherry tomatoes

1 cup (240ml) whole-milk ricotta

1 medium clove garlic, minced

¼ cup (15g) minced fresh flat-leaf parsley

¼ teaspoon salt

Zest of 1 lemon

½ teaspoon fresh lemon juice

1 (8-ounce / 225-g) log goat cheese, pinched into large chunks

Bread or crackers, for serving

DIRECTIONS

1 Preheat the oven to 350°F (175°C). Lightly oil a 5- to 6-inch (12.5- to 15-cm) baking dish.

2 In a small bowl, combine 1 tablespoon of the oil with the tomatoes. Set aside.

3 In a medium bowl, mix together the ricotta, garlic, remaining 2 tablespoons oil, parsley, salt, lemon zest, and lemon juice.

4 Fold the goat cheese into the ricotta mixture.

5 In the baking dish, layer half of the cheese mixture, then add half of the tomatoes. Layer the remaining cheese mixture, then top with the remaining tomatoes. Gently press the top layer of tomatoes into the cheese mixture.

6 Bake, uncovered, until the cheese is melted and the tomatoes are evenly roasted, 25 to 40 minutes. (Cooking time will depend on the thickness of the tomato skins and the depth of the baking dish.)

7 Serve warm with bread or crackers.

ROASTED CHERRY TOMATO AND GOAT CHEESE DIP PAGE 45

summer cream of tomato soup

SERVES 6 TO 8

Beginning in the waning months of winter, one phrase repeatedly gets uttered: "I can't wait for our summer tomatoes." Nothing compares to the flavor of in-season tomatoes, and this soup is designed to feature that amazing taste. The tender, flavorful tomatoes are barely cooked, allowing their sun-infused flavor to shine. If your tomatoes are a bit off-season or are fairly firm, you'll want to simmer them longer (about thirty minutes) before blending and probably add a touch more brown sugar.

INGREDIENTS

2 tablespoons olive oil

2 stalks celery, diced

½ large sweet onion, diced

8 pounds (3.6kg) tomatoes, cut into large chunks

1 cup (240ml) vegetable or chicken stock (may substitute water)

¼ cup (15g) chopped fresh flat-leaf parsley

2 tablespoons chopped fresh basil

2 tablespoons unsalted butter

2 tablespoons flour

3 tablespoons brown sugar

1 tablespoon salt

½ cup (120ml) heavy cream

½ cup (120ml) milk

Fresh thyme, for garnish

DIRECTIONS

1 In a large pot, heat the oil over medium heat. Add the celery and onion and cook until soft, about 5 minutes. Add the tomatoes, stock, parsley, and basil. Stir to combine.

2 Raise the heat to medium-high and bring the mixture to a simmer, then reduce the heat to medium and cook for 10 minutes. Remove the pot from the heat. In batches, transfer the mixture to a blender and blend until smooth. (Be careful—the mixture will be hot.) Strain through a sieve into a large, clean pot.

3 In a small saucepan, melt the butter over medium-high heat. Whisk in the flour, stirring frequently. Continue to cook until the mixture is golden brown and has a slightly nutty aroma.

4 Heat the pureed tomato mixture to a simmer over medium-high heat. Ladle 1 cup (240 ml) of the mixture into the flour-butter mixture and whisk to combine. Pour this back into the pot of the pureed tomato mixture and stir to combine. Simmer for 5 minutes.

5 Add the brown sugar, salt, cream, and milk, then taste for seasoning. Add additional brown sugar and/or salt to taste. Garnish with a sprig of thyme, and serve hot.

baked eggs in tomatoes

SERVES 4

Breakfast is our favorite meal. It's the meal that fuels our long days, and the quiet morning moments in the kitchen allow us to slowly wake up together. Combining our love of eggs and tomatoes, this dish is a highlight for those cooler mornings when we crave something warm from the oven.

The texture of the cooked egg changes in a matter of minutes; cooking time will vary greatly depending on how soft the tomatoes are. Insert a toothpick into the egg to check for your preferred consistency. You may need to use medium-grade eggs rather than large if your tomatoes are on the small side. You can also take out some of the whites when you're filling the tomatoes if the egg volume is too large.

INGREDIENTS

4 medium tomatoes, tops removed and cores cut out

Olive oil, for brushing

4 eggs, medium or large size, depending on size of tomatoes (see above), at room temperature

¼ cup (15g) chopped fresh flat-leaf parsley

¼ cup (25g) freshly grated Parmesan

Kosher or sea salt and freshly cracked black pepper

NOTE If the cored tomatoes are watery, place them upside down on a paper towel to drain.

DIRECTIONS

1 Preheat the oven to 350°F (175°C). Line a sheet pan with parchment paper. Make 4 small rings with crumpled foil as seats for the tomatoes and place the rings on the lined sheet pans.

2 Brush the top edges and outsides of the tomatoes with oil. (If the tomatoes are large and thick skinned, pre-bake them for 5 minutes.)

3 Crack one egg into each tomato. Sprinkle parsley and Parmesan on top. Season with salt and pepper. Place tomatoes on their foil "seats" on the prepared sheet pans.

4 Bake the tomatoes for 25 to 35 minutes, or until the egg is cooked to the desired consistency. Pierce the egg with a fork or toothpick to test its consistency.

PICNIC PASTA SALAD WITH ROASTED TOMATO AND TUNA PAGE 54

picnic pasta salad
with roasted tomato and tuna

SERVES 4

The fragrant aroma and soft, saucelike texture of slow-roasted tomatoes adds great dimension to this humble pasta salad. The mashed tomatoes help bind all the flavors together into a large bowl of comfort. Roast your favorite tomatoes of any shape or size, including cherry tomatoes, and if you want to make the dish extra pretty, use a collage of different tomato colors.

INGREDIENTS

2 pounds (910g) fresh tomatoes

4 tablespoons (60ml) olive oil, plus more for brushing

½ teaspoon kosher or sea salt, plus more for sprinkling

Freshly cracked black pepper

1 medium onion, minced

2 large cloves garlic, minced

2 (5-ounce / 142-g) cans tuna packed in oil, drained

1 pound (455g) fusilli pasta

¼ cup (15g) minced fresh flat-leaf parsley

1 cup (150g) crumbled feta cheese

Zest of 1 lemon

1 tablespoon fresh lemon juice

DIRECTIONS

1 Preheat the oven to 400°F (205°C).

2 Place the tomatoes on a sheet pan and brush them with oil. Sprinkle with salt and pepper to taste.

3 Roast the tomatoes until soft, about 25 minutes. (Roasting time will vary depending on the size and ripeness of the tomatoes.) Allow the tomatoes to cool, then quarter them and remove their seeds, if desired. Cut the quarters into small chunks. Set aside. (If the tomato skins are tough, remove them after roasting.)

4 In a pan, heat 2 tablespoons of the oil over medium heat. Add the onion and garlic and cook until soft. Remove from the heat.

5 Add the tuna to the pan with the onion and garlic and stir to combine. Allow to cool.

6 Cook the fusilli according to the package directions and drain. Place the cooked fusilli in a large bowl.

7 Add the roasted tomatoes, tuna mixture, the ½ teaspoon salt, the parsley, feta cheese, lemon zest, lemon juice, and the remaining 2 tablespoons oil to the bowl with the fusilli.

8 Stir the mixture well to combine. Serve warm or cold.

zesty green tomato pickles

MAKES 1 QUART (1L)

Green globes of tomatoes hanging on the vines are always such a beautiful sight to see. Different shapes, shades, and sizes of green tomatoes pop up everywhere all summer long and will linger into early fall. During the early part of summer, when we're too impatient to wait for these tomatoes to turn their signature red hues, we'll pluck a few pounds and cook them while they're still green. And late in the fall, when the weather begins to turn cool, there are sometimes green tomatoes still on the vines that don't stand a chance of ripening—but will be great in a green tomato recipe. A batch of these zesty, garlicky green tomato pickles are a great accompaniment to sandwiches or grilled dishes, or wonderful just to snack on by themselves. This recipe is just one way we make sure no tomato goes to waste.

INGREDIENTS

About 1 pound (455g) green
  tomatoes

FOR THE BRINE
1½ tablespoons kosher or sea salt
1 teaspoon sugar
2 medium cloves garlic, minced
½ teaspoon celery salt
½ teaspoon caraway seeds
¼ cup (5g) chopped fresh dill
Zest of 1 lime
2 teaspoons fresh lime juice

DIRECTIONS

1 Slice the tomatoes. Stack the slices in sterilized jars (see Note).

2 In a large bowl, combine all the brine ingredients with 3 cups (720ml) water. Stir well, until the salt and sugar have dissolved.

3 Pour the brine into the jars to cover the tomatoes, leaving ¼ inch (6mm) of headspace.

4 Store the tomatoes in the fridge for at least 1 week before eating. The tomatoes will keep in the fridge for up to 3 months, so long as no mold, scum, or spoiling occurs. Check the jars regularly.

NOTE A quick and easy way to sterilize jars is to place them in a pot of hot water, bring the water to a boil, and boil for 10 minutes.

homemade barbecue sauce from fresh tomatoes

MAKES ABOUT 1 PINT

Few things complete a cookout like a homemade barbecue sauce. It is one of those items we always keep on hand. And due to the natural acidity of the sauce, it will store exceptionally well in the fridge. This recipe exhibits our preferred balance between tang, sweetness, and spice. However, it is easy to make adjustments to your own personal taste, as well as to compensate for the flavors of different tomatoes. Add a little more vinegar for tang, a little more brown sugar for sweetness, and a little more hot sauce for heat.

INGREDIENTS

3 pounds (1.4kg) tomatoes

½ medium sweet onion, chopped

3 cloves garlic, crushed

½ cup (120ml) apple cider vinegar

1 tablespoon spicy brown mustard

¼ cup (55g) brown sugar

1 tablespoon fresh lemon juice

3 tablespoons Worcestershire sauce

1 teaspoon soy sauce

1 tablespoon molasses

½ tablespoon Homemade Sriracha (page 196) or other hot sauce

DIRECTIONS

1 In a large pot, combine all the ingredients. Bring the mixture to a simmer over medium heat, then lower the heat to low and simmer for 30 minutes, or until the tomatoes are very soft. Remove the sauce from the heat and allow to cool.

2 In a blender, puree the sauce until smooth. Add water as needed if you desire a thinner sauce. Strain the sauce through a sieve and pour it into sterilized jars (see Note, page 55), leaving ¼ inch (6mm) of head-space. Allow the sauce to cool completely, then store it in the refrigerator for up to one month.

3 For longer storage, can the sauce-filled jars in a water bath: Put the sealed jars in a large pot. Fill the pot with water to 1 inch (2.5 cm) above the jars, and bring the water to a simmer. Simmer for 15 minutes. Remove the jars from the water and allow to cool. Store the sealed jars for up to 6 months.

red tomato jam with fresh ginger

MAKES ABOUT 2 CUPS (480ML)

Appreciating tomatoes as both fruits and vegetables opens up our minds to the endless possibilities of cooking with them. When tomatoes are plentiful, we add their sweet fruitiness to our repertoire of jams and preserves. Delicately spiced with warm, earthy flavors, this red tomato jam is a welcome change from our berry jams. A generous swipe of tomato jam on warm toast with a fragrant cup of coffee remind us how great a simple summer-morning breakfast can be.

INGREDIENTS

2 pounds (910g) ripe tomatoes, roughly chopped

½ cup (110g) packed brown sugar

1½ tablespoons grated or finely minced fresh ginger

¼ teaspoon ground cloves

1 teaspoon ground cinnamon

2 teaspoons apple cider vinegar

2 teaspoons fresh lime juice

DIRECTIONS

1 In a saucepan, combine all the ingredients and bring to a boil over medium-high heat, stirring well.

2 Reduce the heat to low and simmer, stirring occasionally and gently, until the mixture thickens to a jamlike consistency, about 1 hour.

3 Remove the jam from the heat and allow to cool.

4 Pour the jam into sterilized jars (see Note, page 55), leaving ¼ inch (6mm) of headspace. The jam will keep for up to one month. For longer storage, can the jam jars in a water bath: Put the sealed jars in a large pot. Fill the pot with water to 1 inch (2.5 cm) above the jars, and bring the water to a simmer. Simmer for 15 minutes. Remove the jars from the water and allow to cool. Store the sealed jars for up to 1 year.

RED TOMATO JAM WITH FRESH GINGER PAGE 59

herbs & leafy greens

OUR VERY FIRST GARDEN TOGETHER WAS A collection of small terra-cotta pots filled with fragrant herbs and baby greens. Our tiny green space was cultivated on the second-story balcony of an apartment that we shared with two other roommates. These leaves not only fed us in the kitchen, but also nourished our spirits. They were the easiest plants to grow on our space-challenged little patio, and they brought us so much satisfaction. As long as we remembered to water them on hot summer days, we would have meals laced with the most tender herbaceous leaves. If we forgot the watering duties, then we had brown, crumbly twigs of freshly dried herbs. This was one of the many growing pains of learning to garden in small pots. But in the end we still felt successful because there was always an herb element to cook with and some small microgreens to eat.

When we finally bought a home with real gardening space, the first things we planted (right next to the kitchen door) were herbs we frequently used. Their ability to transform a recipe is unparalleled; a few leaves can turn a dish from ordinary to amazing. Sprigs of mint, thyme, basil, oregano, rosemary, and Vietnamese herbs have always made our cooking more layered in flavor. Whether added to enhance the freshness of an already exciting salad or rubbed into a roasted dish, the herbs fill the kitchen with their warm, earthy aromas.

You'll always find a component of fresh leafy greens at our daily meals. The crisp bite of a bed of lettuce leaves us feeling satisfied and complete. Summer also means a plethora of handheld foods made with the season's baby lettuces in a variety of colors and lacy textures. Sweet, delicate leaves are used to bundle chicken and other savory delights into lettuce wraps. When we're satisfied with those, we move on to wrapping the leaves into a multitude of different spring rolls.

Without herbs and lettuces, Vietnamese dishes wouldn't have their traditional layering of crunchy greens or their trademark flair of freshness. If we had to single out the ingredients most crucial to our kitchen garden, it would be the fresh herbs and leafy greens.

If you live in a tiny apartment or feel you don't have a green thumb, try nurturing a few pots of herbs and lettuce seedlings on your windowsill. If you're able to harvest a few handfuls of leaves for your next dish, you can consider yourself a successful gardener. It's not the quantity of what your garden grows that's important. What matters most is the joy and satisfaction that even the tiniest of nature's leaves can bring.

herbed garlic knots

MAKES ABOUT 40 KNOTS

From Todd These take me back to my days of working in the restaurant business. Every day the kitchen would crank out a huge basket of garlic knots that we'd sell throughout the day. Those little devils would also serve as staff sustenance, since more often than not, breaks were skipped in order to get the day's tasks done. Even after consuming what seems like a thousand garlic knots, I have never tired of snacking on them to get me through a long day. After leaving the restaurant business, that daily ritual inspired me to create my own version, and they are as addicting as ever.

It is not necessary to knead this dough; that will only toughen it. When you're rolling the dough, lightly oil the surface you roll on to help the dough stick just enough, and lightly flour your hands and the dough balls to keep them from sticking too much. Find the balance between the two for best results.

INGREDIENTS

FOR THE DOUGH
1¾ cups (420ml) warm water (about 115°F / 46°C)

¼ cup (60ml) olive oil, plus more for brushing

1 teaspoon kosher or sea salt

1 tablespoon sugar

1½ tablespoons active dry yeast

About 5½ cups (685g) flour, plus more for rolling

FOR THE GARLIC-HERB COATING
¼ cup (60ml) olive oil

¼ cup (½ stick / 57g) unsalted butter

6 medium cloves garlic, finely chopped

⅓ cup (20g) finely chopped fresh flat-leaf parsley

Kosher or sea salt

DIRECTIONS

1 **Make the dough:** In a large sealable container or bowl, combine the water, oil, salt, sugar, and yeast. Mix to dissolve the yeast.

2 Mix in the flour, cover, and set in a warm area to proof until doubled in volume, 1 to 3 hours, depending on initial water temperature and warmth of proofing area.

3 Chill the dough until ready to make knots, at least 1 hour and up to several days.

4 **Set up a rolling station:** Heavily flour a board to hold the dough balls. Lightly oil a second board for forming ropes of dough to knot. Line several sheet pans with parchment paper.

5 Pinch off dough balls the size of ping pong balls (about 1 ounce / 30g each) and set them on the floured board.

6 Knock off excess flour one dough ball at a time, then roll the ball back and forth between your hands and against the oiled board to create an even rope 7 inches (17.5 cm) long.
recipe continues

HERB-CRUSTED SALMON PAGE 67
BRAISED BRUSSELS SPROUTS PAGE 117

basil pesto farro salad

SERVES 4

Our love of farro has no end, and it's a staple whole grain in our pantry. Farro's nuttiness adds wonderful flavor and texture to salads. A simple mix of fresh basil pesto and farro is a satisfying cold salad perfect for a quick afternoon lunch or a picnic gathering. Consider adding other crunchy elements to this salad, such as nuts, chopped celery, and cucumber.

INGREDIENTS

1 cup (200g) raw farro

¼ cup (60ml) Fresh Herb Pesto (page 72)

1 medium red bell pepper, chopped small

⅔ cup (100g) crumbled feta cheese

Kosher or sea salt and freshly cracked black pepper

1 bunch of radish bulbs, sliced

DIRECTIONS

1 In a saucepan, combine the farro with 2½ cups (600ml) water. Bring to a simmer, cover, then reduce the heat to low and simmer for 25 minutes or until the water is fully absorbed. Remove from the heat and allow to cool.

2 In a bowl, combine the cooked farro, pesto, bell pepper, and feta cheese.

3 Add salt and pepper to taste.

4 Top with the sliced radishes before serving.

fresh herb pesto

MAKES ABOUT 2 CUPS (480ML)

The transition from late spring to early summer is when our herbs explode with fragrant, tender leaves. Gathering herbs at this time of year is always a treat because the oils and soft stems are at their peak, and that means making pesto of all different kinds. Basil pesto is always a favorite, but other herbs, such as thyme, mint, tarragon, and even arugula, prove to be wonderful variations as well. Consider mixing up your own unique batch of pesto with various herbs and nuts, including walnuts, peanuts, and cashews.

INGREDIENTS

¼ cup (34g) pine nuts

15 walnut halves, or ¼ cup (25g) nuts of your choice

4 whole black peppercorns

2 medium cloves garlic

4 cups (100g) fresh basil leaves, or herb leaves of your choice

2 cups (200g) freshly grated Parmesan

1 tablespoon fresh lemon juice

1 teaspoon kosher or sea salt

1 cup (240ml) extra-virgin olive oil

DIRECTIONS

1 In a food processor, combine the pine nuts, walnut halves, peppercorns, and garlic. Pulse a few times to break up and combine the ingredients.

2 Add the basil, Parmesan, lemon juice, salt, and ½ cup (120ml) of the oil to the food processor and process until very fine.

3 Gradually add the remaining oil, to taste, pulsing until smooth (you may not need the full amount of oil, depending on your preferred texture for the pesto).

rosemary lemonade

MAKES 6 CUPS (1.4 L)

Wander through our garden and you'll realize that many of the big hedges we're clipping from are actually bushes of rosemary. This savory herb transforms the empty corners of our garden into beautiful landscapes and fills our meals with wonderful flavors. The delicate infusion of a few rosemary sprigs in a pitcher of refreshing lemonade makes a classic drink extra-special.

INGREDIENTS

½ cup (120ml) fresh lemon juice

1 cup (240ml) Simple Syrup (recipe follows), cooled

2 sprigs fresh rosemary

Ice

DIRECTIONS

In a pitcher, combine all the ingredients with 4 cups (960ml) water. Add a few rinds from the freshly squeezed lemons and stir to combine. Serve over ice.

SIMPLE SYRUP

MAKES ABOUT 3 CUPS (720ML)

This is our basic simple syrup recipe. We'll often make variations by substituting palm sugar or agave nectar for some of the granulated sugar, or by infusing ginger or mint into the syrup while it is boiling. It is great for making your own sodas by adding it to soda water.

2 cups (480ml) water
2 cups (400g) sugar

In a medium saucepan, combine the ingredients. Stir and bring to a simmer. Simmer for 15 to 20 seconds, then remove from the heat. Allow to cool. Transfer to a sterilized jar (see Note, page 55) and store in the refrigerator for up to 3 weeks.

mussels steamed
with herbs and white wine

SERVES 2

Any time we have mussels, we think of traveling through the Pacific Northwest. The mussels we've had there have been incredible: plump and meaty, with great texture. It is usually just the two of us, bundled up against the cold, huddling over the steamy broth, popping open the shells, making sure to have a bit of the broth in the mussel, then slurping down the mussel and broth together. In this recipe, the tarragon and parsley lend a refreshing bouquet to the broth. If you are a fan of licorice, add star anise to bring out that flavor from the tarragon.

INGREDIENTS

2 tablespoons unsalted butter

2 tablespoons finely chopped shallots

3 medium garlic cloves, crushed or minced

1 star anise (optional)

1½ cups (360ml) dry white wine

3 tablespoons chopped fresh tarragon

1 tablespoon chopped fresh flat-leaf parsley

2 pounds (910g) mussels, scrubbed and debearded

Grilled or toasted crusty bread (French fries, or *pommes frites*, are also a classic companion)

DIRECTIONS

1 In a large pot, melt the butter over medium heat. Add the shallots, garlic, and star anise, if using. Cook for 1 minute, or until the garlic and shallots are soft.

2 Add the wine, tarragon, and parsley and bring to a simmer. Add the mussels. Cover and simmer for 3 minutes. Stir and cook for 2 more minutes, or until most of the mussels have opened up.

3 Remove the mussels from the pot and place them in a serving bowl, discarding any mussels that haven't opened. Pour the broth over the mussels and serve accompanied by the bread or *pommes frites*.

MUSSELS STEAMED WITH HERBS AND WHITE WINE PAGE 75

peppermint chocolate chip ice cream

MAKES ABOUT 1 QUART (1L)

We first grew peppermint in the garden for one purpose: mint chocolate chip ice cream. It is such a bright mint that its culinary use is more limited than the milder spearmint. When mellowed out by cream and milk, however, it is amazing. Make sure not to substitute milk chocolate chips for the dark chocolate. They just don't work as well.

INGREDIENTS

1½ cups (360ml) heavy cream

1 cup (240ml) milk

½ cup (100g) sugar

Pinch of kosher or sea salt

Peppermint leaves from
   15 (6-inch / 15-cm) stems

5 egg yolks

5 ounces (140g) dark chocolate,
   finely chopped

SPECIAL EQUIPMENT
Ice cream machine

ALTERNATE METHOD If your ice cream machine makes it difficult to drizzle the chocolate in while the machine is churning the ice cream, you can also add the chocolate to the ice cream after it is done churning. Drizzle some of the chocolate over the ice cream, then fold and layer the ice cream through the chocolate streaks, breaking up chunks of chocolate as you stir. Continue drizzling the chocolate and folding the ice cream through the chocolate until the chocolate is fully chipped into the ice cream.

DIRECTIONS

1 In a saucepan over medium heat, combine the cream, milk, sugar, and salt, stirring to dissolve the sugar. Bring to a bare simmer, stirring frequently. Add the peppermint leaves. Remove the pan from the heat and cover. Set aside for 30 minutes.

2 In a medium bowl, whisk the egg yolks. Strain the cream mixture through a sieve and discard the peppermint leaves. Slowly whisk the cream mixture into the egg yolks. Pour the mixture back into the saucepan and turn the heat to medium, stirring constantly and scraping the bottom as you stir. Cook until the mixture thickens enough to coat the back of a spatula or wooden spoon (1 to 2 minutes after reaching a bare simmer).

3 Pour the custard through a fine-mesh sieve into a clean container. Place the container in an ice bath, stirring the custard occasionally until it is cool, about 20 minutes. Cover and refrigerate for at least 2 hours, or overnight.

4 When ready to freeze, set a completely dry heat-proof bowl over a pot of simmering water and melt the chocolate. Stir until the chocolate is completely smooth, then remove the pot from the heat.
recipe continues

5 Freeze the custard according to the ice cream machine directions. While churning the ice cream, place the container in which you will store it in the freezer to chill.

6 In the last few moments of churning, drizzle a fine stream of the chocolate into the ice cream with the machine on. Make sure to drizzle only into the ice cream, not onto the dasher (mixing blade). Transfer the ice cream from the ice cream machine into the chilled storage container. Store the ice cream in the freezer until ready to serve.

spinach and bacon salad
with avocado vinaigrette

SERVES 3 TO 4

Fresh, tender spinach, avocado, and bacon tossed together in a bowl is a marriage of some of our favorite ingredients. When new spinach comes up in the garden or when the farmer's markets display their big bins of greens, it's hard not to crave a big bowl of this wonderful combination for dinner.

We first started to grow spinach by tossing a few seeds in a wine barrel that was used as a planter. Within a few weeks, we had the most incredible spinach greens. Now we're addicted and eagerly await the first spinach crop of every season. For this recipe, we show our love of avocados too, by doubling up on them: one for the vinaigrette, and the other cut into chunks and added to the salad. And of course you can always add more bacon if you like.

INGREDIENTS

FOR THE VINAIGRETTE

¼ cup (60ml) olive oil or neutral-flavor oil such as grapeseed

1 tablespoon balsamic vinegar

1 tablespoon fresh lemon juice

1 teaspoon soy sauce

½ teaspoon brown sugar

1 medium avocado, peeled, pitted, and diced

FOR THE SALAD

1 bunch fresh spinach, roughly chopped

6 strips bacon, cooked and crumbled

¼ cup (23g) almonds, sliced and toasted

1 medium avocado, peeled, pitted, and cubed

1 medium tomato, chopped (optional)

DIRECTIONS

1 **Make the vinaigrette:** In a medium bowl or Mason jar, whisk the vinaigrette ingredients (except for the avocado) until well combined. Mix the avocado into the vinaigrette. You can keep the avocado diced or mash it into the dressing for a creamy texture.

2 **Make the salad:** Place the spinach in a large salad bowl.

3 Add the vinaigrette to the spinach and toss well. Then gently mix in the bacon, almonds, avocado, and tomato (if using) right before serving.

lettuce wraps
with almond-basil chicken

SERVES 4

Rarely are we without a head of lettuce in the fridge or a new batch of lettuce seedlings in the garden. Lettuce is the starter or base for many of our meals, particularly those with Asian-inspired menus. Our Vietnamese noodle salads or wraps will always be accompanied by a huge platter of raw lettuce, and often the lettuce dish is the decorative centerpiece of the table. In this versatile recipe, you can substitute shrimp, beef, pork, tofu, or chopped vegetables for the chicken.

INGREDIENTS

2 tablespoons grapeseed oil or other cooking oil

1 small onion, minced

2 medium cloves garlic, minced

1 pound (455g) chicken cutlets, diced small

1 small red bell pepper, halved, seeded, and diced

1 teaspoon honey

2 teaspoons fish sauce or soy sauce

2 tablespoons hoisin sauce

½ teaspoon rice vinegar

1 head fresh lettuce leaves, broadleaf variety, for wrapping

½ cup (20g) chopped fresh basil

¼ cup (23g) roasted almonds, sliced

DIRECTIONS

1 In a large sauté pan, heat the oil over medium heat. Add the onion and garlic and cook until soft.

2 Add the chicken and cook until browned, about 5 minutes.

3 Stir in the bell pepper, honey, fish sauce, hoisin sauce, and rice vinegar. Continue cooking until the chicken is fully cooked, 10 to 15 minutes.

4 Serve the chicken in a shallow dish alongside a plate of the lettuce leaves. Fill the leaves with the chicken mixture, and top with a sprinkling of basil and almonds.

creamed swiss chard
in goat cheese on baked potatoes

SERVES 6

A generous dollop of sour cream always makes its way onto our baked potatoes. But recently, we've been craving a vegetable version of this treat, and gorgeous Swiss chard is the perfect option. Creamed Swiss chard in goat cheese satisfies our craving for something creamy-rich on top of baked potatoes, but it also adds the wonderful texture and flavor of a chewy green. It's our way of including a great vegetable with our potatoes, while at the same time being a little indulgent. Life is about balance, and these baked potatoes are a great example of it—well, at least a culinary one!

INGREDIENTS

3 medium potatoes

1 tablespoon unsalted butter

1 large shallot, minced

1 pound (455g) Swiss chard, ribs and tough stems removed, leaves roughly chopped

2 tablespoons heavy cream

¼ cup (60g) goat cheese

¼ teaspoon kosher or sea salt

Freshly cracked black pepper, to taste

DIRECTIONS

1 Preheat the oven to 350°F (175°C). Pierce each potato several times with a fork, and wrap them individually in aluminum foil. Bake for 45 minutes, or until well cooked on the inside.

2 In a large pan, heat the butter over medium heat. Add the shallot and cook until soft.

3 Add the Swiss chard and cook until wilted.

4 Add the cream, goat cheese, salt, and pepper. Cook, stirring occasionally to combine, until the cheese is completely melted, about 3 minutes.

5 Cut the baked potatoes in half and spoon the hot creamed chard over the tops.

creamed dill chicken potpie with puff pastry

SERVES 6 TO 8

Until recently, dill was an underappreciated herb in our garden. We would mostly grow it for its delicate structure and because it was a favorite of the swallowtail butterfly caterpillars. It wasn't until we had dill in a cream sauce with chicken, accented by a touch of mustard, that we started making sure we grew enough for the caterpillars *and* ourselves. Take that creamed dill chicken and encase it in puff pastry for a potpie, and it becomes perfect comfort food. Over the winter, grow some dill in your windowsill, or if you are lucky enough to live in a temperate area like Southern California, make sure to grow dill in the cool months. But be forewarned: You may find yourself addicted.

INGREDIENTS

2 pounds (910g) boneless, skinless chicken (thighs or breasts)

Salt and freshly cracked black pepper

½ cup (1 stick / 113g) unsalted butter, divided

4 medium shallots, sliced

4 medium cloves garlic, crushed or minced

½ pound (225g) carrots, cut into ½-inch (12-mm) pieces

2 cups (330g) fresh corn kernels (from about 2 ears)

½ cup (120ml) dry white wine

2 tablespoons brandy

¼ cup (30g) flour

1 cup (240ml) heavy cream, plus more for brushing the pastry

1 cup (240ml) chicken stock

1 tablespoon grainy mustard

¼ cup (5g) minced dill

1 pound (455g) Puff Pastry Dough (page 284)

DIRECTIONS

1 Preheat the oven to 400°F (205°C).

2 Rinse the chicken and pat it dry. If the chicken pieces are thick, place them between two sheets of plastic wrap and lightly pound them to ½ inch (12 mm) thick. Season the pieces with salt and pepper.

3 In a large sauté pan, melt 2 tablespoons of the butter over medium-high heat. Add the chicken and cook until lightly browned, about 4 minutes on each side. Remove the chicken from the pan and set aside to cool.

4 To the same pan, add 1 tablespoon of the butter, then add the shallots, garlic, carrots, and corn and cook over medium heat until the shallots begin to soften, 3 to 5 minutes. Add the wine and brandy and simmer until the pan is almost dry, 12 to 15 minutes.

5 Add the remaining 1 tablespoon butter. When it is melted, stir in the flour. Cook, stirring, for 1 minute, then add the cream and stock. Simmer, stirring occasionally, until thickened, about 5 minutes.

6 Cut the browned chicken into ½-inch (12-mm) pieces and add them to the cream sauce. Add the mustard and dill, then season to taste with salt and pepper.

7 Fill a 2-quart (2-L) baking dish with the dill-chicken mixture. Lightly dust a work surface with flour. Roll the puff pastry out to a sheet large enough to cover the top of the baking dish and filling. Place the puff pastry over the filling, then cut a small slit in the top to allow the steam to vent. Brush the pastry with heavy cream.

8 Bake for 30 minutes, or until the pastry is deep golden. Serve hot.

beans, stalks & shoots

THE CRISP SNAP OF A SWEET PEA OR A STALK of baby asparagus is like music heralding the arrival of spring. When tender beans, stalks, and shoots start popping up above ground and at the markets, we know the world is coming out of winter hibernation.

For us, a simple springtime breakfast includes a handful of fresh sugar snap peas plucked from their dew-dripping vines and tendrils. These short, plump green pearls taste like crisp candy and make us feel like giggly kids for that part of the day.

Because peas are so plentiful on the vine, they're made for sharing. We consider them the community vegetable; they give us the ability to feed our neighbors, our friends, and even our mailman. These are vegetables to brighten up everyone's days.

To extend this wonderful season of beans and shoots, we immediately start the pickling process and set aside a few jars of pickled beans or asparagus to savor toward the end of the year. Our quick-pickled sugar snap peas infused with mint are always a sign that we're embracing spring's peak.

If you're inclined to take pickling a few steps further, try making a batch of pickled celery using the same pickling brine as the quick pea pickles on page 100. You'll be pleased at how fresh and delicious the savory crunch of celery can be alongside an afternoon sandwich.

Our affection for rhubarb also grows by the season. Pies, tarts, and preserves studded with its brilliant hues are not only pleasing to our eyes, but also bring pleasure to our bellies. Our latest crush on rhubarb is in the form of a bread pudding, and the recipe is included in this chapter on page 108. You must give this unique bread pudding a try.

Last but not least, a discussion of this group of vegetables would not be complete without mention of fresh baby shoots and tendrils of all kinds. Loaded into salads to replace lettuce, or used as garnish on top of grilled dishes for extra texture, shoots can easily revitalize a sleepy dish.

creamed haricots verts
with toasted almonds

SERVES 4

Regardless of how many side dishes are on the holiday table, someone always asks for creamed green beans. So to make sure everyone is eating happily (yes, we're eager to please), we came up with a simple creamed dish featuring haricots verts, which are more slender, tender, and crisp than traditional green beans.

It sometimes feels a bit tragic to cook thin and tender haricots verts in a thick, creamy sauce. But the holidays are about indulging and spreading joy. So if friends and family ask for this favorite comfort food, we're more than happy to oblige. Besides, it's hard to say no to anything topped with fresh Parmesan. (We prefer to keep this recipe simple, but you can always add fried onions to please the onion lovers at the table!)

INGREDIENTS

1 tablespoon olive oil

1 medium onion, sliced

1 pound (455g) haricots verts or small green beans, trimmed and cut into 2-inch (5-cm) pieces

2 ounces (55g) cream cheese

½ cup (50g) freshly grated Parmesan, plus more for serving

¾ cup (180ml) milk

½ teaspoon kosher or sea salt

¼ cup (23g) toasted sliced almonds

DIRECTIONS

1 In a large pan, heat the oil over medium heat. Add the onion and cook until soft and lightly browned.

2 Add the haricots verts and cook until they turn a bright green color, 2 to 3 minutes.

3 While stirring, add the cream cheese, Parmesan, milk, and salt. Cook until the cream cheese melts completely and the beans are tender, about 5 minutes. Serve warm, topped with extra Parmesan and the almonds.

tender roasted green beans
with walnuts and feta

SERVES 4

Our picnics and potlucks usually include some sort of green bean recipe. Green bean salads such as this one hold up well at such gatherings—they're tremendously popular and easy to eat. Our variation is very tender, because we take an extra step and quickly blanch the green beans. Green beans can often be dry and tough when roasted, so the quick blanching helps produce a very tender batch of beans. Just make sure to drain the beans very well of any excess water. This recipe is great served hot or cold.

INGREDIENTS

Kosher or sea salt

1 pound (455g) green beans, ends trimmed, cut into 2-inch (5-cm) pieces

2 tablespoons olive oil

1 tablespoon balsamic vinegar

½ cup (60g) chopped walnuts, toasted

2 teaspoons chopped fresh thyme

1 cup (150g) crumbled feta cheese

Zest of ½ lemon (reserve lemon half for squeezing)

DIRECTIONS

1 Preheat the oven to 400°F (205°C).

2 Fill a large pot halfway with water, add a pinch of salt, and bring to a boil. Meanwhile, fill a large bowl with ice water.

3 Add the green beans to the pot and stir until the beans turn a bright green color, about 30 seconds; do not overcook the beans.

4 Immediately drain the beans, then place them in the ice water. Allow the beans to cool completely, then drain well. If needed, blot the beans with a paper towel to remove any excess water.

5 In a large bowl, combine the oil, vinegar, walnuts, salt to taste, and thyme. Add the beans to the bowl and toss to coat. Spread the mixture on a sheet pan.

6 Roast for 10 minutes. Gently stir the mixture and roast for 10 minutes more, or until the beans are tender.

7 Transfer the beans to a serving bowl. Top with the feta cheese, lemon zest, and a squeeze of lemon juice. Serve warm or as a cold salad.

sautéed celery and shrimp

SERVES 4

We're always singing the praises of the humble celery stalk. As much as we enjoy snacking on it raw, this wonderful stalk proves to be equally exceptional sautéed. Two simple ingredients—celery and shrimp—make this a great side dish, or it can be added to rice, noodles, or salad. If you are able to grow celery, you are in for a treat; homegrown stalks are extra tender and flavorful compared to store-bought.

INGREDIENTS

½ pound (225g) shrimp, peeled and deveined

2 teaspoons vegetable oil, plus 1 tablespoon

2 teaspoons fish sauce

1 teaspoon sugar

Freshly cracked black pepper

8 stalks celery, sliced crosswise

Kosher or sea salt

DIRECTIONS

1 In a large bowl, combine the shrimp, 2 teaspoons of the oil, the fish sauce, sugar, and pepper to taste. Gently toss to coat the shrimp.

2 Heat a sauté pan over high heat. When the pan is very hot, swirl in the remaining 1 tablespoon oil. Add the celery and cook for 1 minute, stirring occasionally.

3 Add the shrimp and cook for 1 minute. Flip the shrimp and cook for 1 minute more, or until pink.

4 Season with salt to taste and serve warm.

crispy soybean fritters

SERVES 2 TO 3

From Diane During my almost twenty years as a vegetarian, I craved beans and legumes for protein. I ate almost every variety of bean I could find, but my favorite was—and still remains—soybeans (edamame). They're meaty and have a great, satisfying bite. These patties are great as a side dish or as additions to salads, or if made into wider patties, they make great burgers.

The key to success with this recipe is to make firm patties before frying. They will hold their shape and are less likely to fall apart. When frying, just use a small amount of oil at a time, as needed, and don't let the skillet get too hot, or else the bread crumbs will burn before the inside of the fritter is cooked.

INGREDIENTS

1 (12-ounce / 340-g) package frozen shelled soybeans (edamame), thawed

½ cup (120ml) milk

1 egg yolk

¼ teaspoon soy sauce, plus more for serving

½ cup (55g) bread crumbs

Vegetable oil

Finely chopped fresh cilantro or mint, for garnish (optional)

DIRECTIONS

1 In a blender, combine the soybeans and milk. Slowly pulse to coarsely chop the soybeans. Continue pulsing, scraping the sides of the blender with a rubber spatula occasionally, until the mixture is coarsely mashed. Pour the mixture into a medium bowl.

2 Add the egg yolk, ¼ teaspoon soy sauce, and 1 tablespoon of the bread crumbs. Mix well. Scoop out about 2 tablespoons at a time, and use your hands to press the soybean mixture into patties about 2 inches (5 cm) in diameter.

3 In a large skillet, heat 2 tablespoons of oil over medium heat.

4 Place the remaining bread crumbs in a small bowl. Gently place the patties in the bowl and coat them thoroughly on all sides with the bread crumbs.

5 Fry the patties in batches until crispy and light golden, about 2 minutes on each side, or until crispy. Transfer the finished patties to a parchment-paper-covered wire rack. Continue to add small amounts of oil to the pan, as needed, to fry each batch. These patties can be very fragile, so flip and transfer gently.

6 Serve with soy sauce, or garnish with cilantro or mint.

QUICK PICKLED SUGAR SNAP PEAS WITH MINT PAGE 100

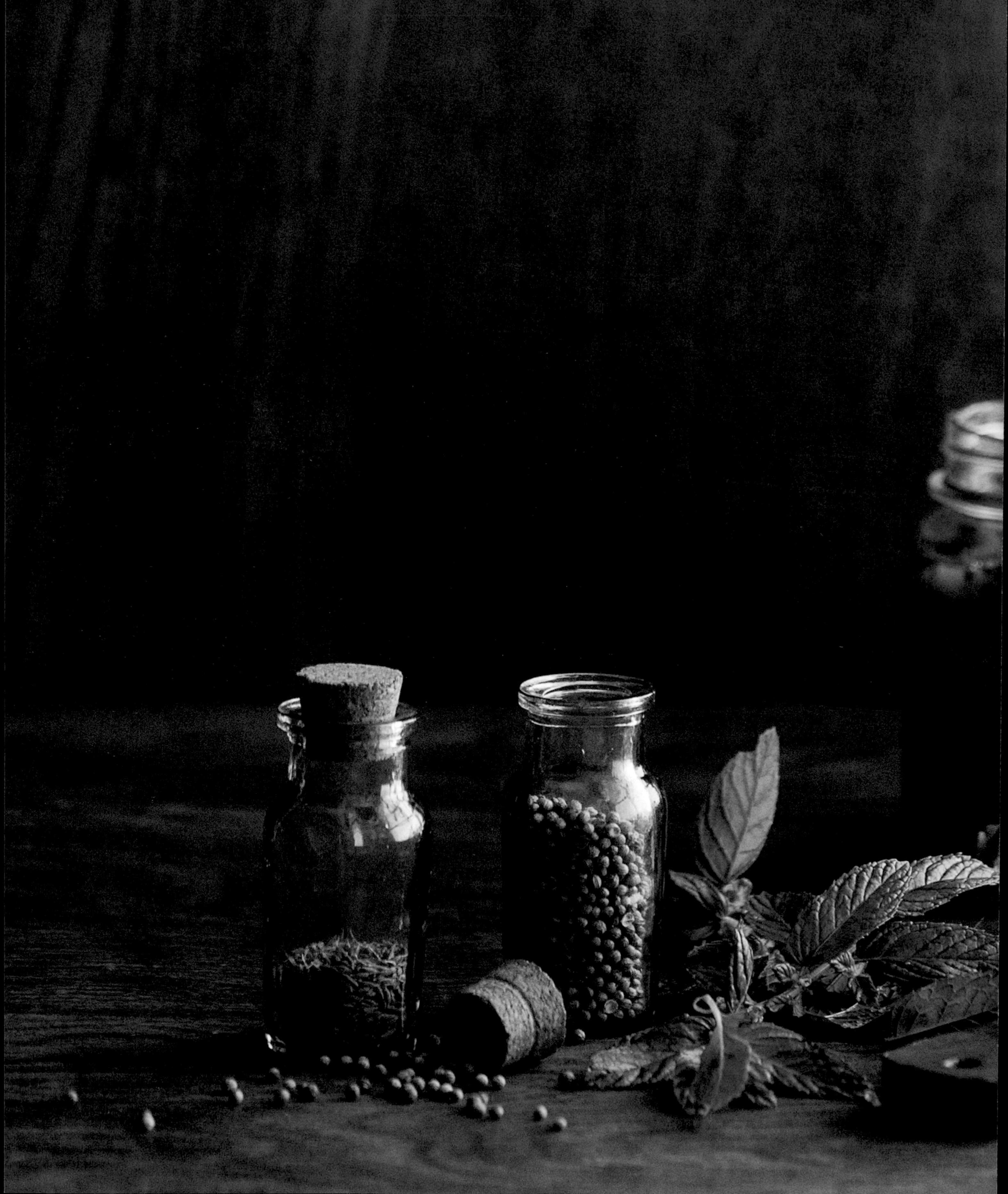

6 **Make the filling:** In a saucepan, heat the milk, cream, and bay leaf to a scald (just until a skin begins to form on the surface). Remove from the heat and let cool for 10 minutes.

7 In a sauté pan, heat the oil over medium heat. Add the cippolini and cook, stirring occasionally, until they are soft, 2 to 3 minutes. Remove from the heat and set aside.

8 Remove the bay leaf from the milk mixture. Whisk in the eggs, fish sauce, and pepper to taste.

9 Using a sharp knife, trim the excess dough from the crust. Arrange the cippolini, asparagus, and goat cheese inside the crust. Pour the milk mixture into the crust.

10 Bake for 35 minutes, or until the filling is barely set in the middle. Let cool for 10 to 15 minutes, then cut the quiche into wedges and serve. The quiche can also be refrigerated, then reheated for 10 to 15 minutes in a 350°F (175°C) oven. It will keep for up to 3 days.

braised artichokes in white wine

SERVES 6

Every year, we get four or five nice-size artichokes in our garden. But when our friends' kids come over, we have watched in horror as the artichokes became balls on a stick for them to play with, or spiky specimens in a game of tetherball. So we've learned our lesson and now make sure we harvest the artichokes before these invaders make their way into the garden.

This recipe is the grand treatment for the artichokes. After the initial braise in an aromatic broth of wine, garlic, and shallots, the artichokes are seared to give an extra layer of flavor and a contrasting texture to their soft hearts. They are so good that each person may eat at least two halves, so plan on making a big batch if you're serving a crowd.

INGREDIENTS

6 medium artichokes

½ lemon

3 tablespoons unsalted butter

3 tablespoons olive oil

4 cloves garlic, crushed

2 medium shallots, peeled and sliced

2 whole bay leaves

1 tablespoon fresh lemon juice

¾ cup (180ml) dry white wine

1 teaspoon kosher or sea salt

DIRECTIONS

1 Cut 1 inch (2.5 cm) off the top of each artichoke. Peel off the tough outer leaves until you reach leaves that are a light yellow. Trim the stem to 1 inch (2.5 cm) from the base of each artichoke. Place the trimmed artichokes in a bowl of water and squeeze juice from the lemon half into the water to prevent browning.

2 In a wide pot, tall enough so the artichokes will be able to stand and the pot can still be covered, melt 2 tablespoons of the butter with 2 tablespoons of the oil over medium heat. Add the garlic and shallots and cook until the shallots are soft, about 5 minutes.

3 Add the bay leaves, lemon juice, wine, ¾ cup (180ml) water, and the salt. Raise the heat and bring the liquid to a simmer. Stand the artichokes, stems pointing up, in the poaching liquid. Cover.

4 Reduce the heat to low and gently simmer for 20 to 30 minutes, or until the stems of the artichokes are tender.

5 Remove the artichokes, reserving the poaching liquid. When the artichokes are cool enough to handle, carefully cut them in half and scoop out the chokes (the fuzzy center parts).

6 Simmer the reserved poaching liquid over high heat until reduced, about 10 minutes.

7 Meanwhile, heat a sauté pan over medium-high heat. Add the remaining tablespoon butter and remaining tablespoon oil. When the butter is melted and no longer bubbling, add the artichokes, cut side down, and sear for 2 to 3 minutes, or until browned.

8 Plate the artichokes and serve drizzled with the reduced poaching liquid.

roasted asparagus spring rolls with bacon

MAKES ABOUT 10 ROLLS

From Diane One of the very first home-cooked meals we shared was a picnic of fresh spring rolls. We didn't have a dining table back then, so I assembled a big platter of cooked vegetables, herbs, lettuce, and rice paper wrappers on the living room floor. Todd learned to roll his first Vietnamese spring rolls, and he quickly learned to roll perfectly tight and plump rolls. It was a bonding moment between us. Fast forward seventeen years, and we still roll and eat spring rolls on a weekly basis, but now we have a table to feast on.

The fillings here are not traditionally Vietnamese, but they are examples of the endless possibilities for spring rolls. This recipe is not paired with a dip because the bacon is already quite salty. If you prefer to have a dip, try the recipes for Garlic Soy Dipping Sauce (see page 108) or Vietnamese Fish Sauce Dressing (see page 124).

INGREDIENTS

1 bunch tender baby asparagus (about ½ pound / 225g)

1 tablespoon olive oil

Freshly cracked black pepper

12 slices bacon, fried

1 cucumber, cut into matchsticks

1 medium carrot, cut into matchsticks (optional)

Lettuce leaves

Fresh basil or mint leaves

Rice paper wrappers

Garlic Soy Dipping Sauce (optional; see page 108)

DIRECTIONS

1 Preheat the oven to 400°F (205°C).

2 Trim any dry or tough ends from the asparagus spears. On a sheet pan, toss the asparagus with the oil. Add pepper to taste. (Do not salt the asparagus because the bacon will be salty.)

3 Roast until tender, 10 to 15 minutes. (Cooking time will vary depending on the size and thickness of the asparagus.)

4 Gather the asparagus, bacon, cucumber, carrot (if using), lettuce leaves, herb leaves, and rice paper wrappers and prepare to roll.

TO ROLL

1 Fill a large bowl with warm (bath-temperature) water. Gently dip each rice paper wrapper in the water for a few seconds, just until damp. (Don't oversoak.) Place the wrapper on a plate or wooden board. As the wrapper begins to absorb the water and becomes softer
recipe continues

7 Layer the remaining bread over the rhubarb. Pour the milk-egg mixture over the bread. Press down gently on the bread to help the top layer absorb the liquids.

8 Set the baking dish aside for 30 minutes to allow the bread to absorb the liquids fully. Layer the remaining rhubarb over top.

9 Preheat the oven to 350°F (175°C).

10 Place the baking dish inside a larger roasting pan and fill the roasting pan with enough water to reach half-way up the side of the bread pudding dish. Bake for 1 hour, or until the pudding is golden brown and set.

11 While the bread pudding is baking, simmer the reserved poaching liquid over high heat until reduced, about 10 minutes. Serve the reduced liquid alongside or drizzled over the bread pudding.

broccoli & other cruciferous vegetables

ON OUR LIST OF GARDENING SKILLS TO improve on, growing Brussels sprouts and cauliflower are at the top. Perhaps it's the warmer weather in our region, but we're not all that good at growing most cruciferous vegetables in the cabbage family—though we are absolutely great at eating them. So when we see gardens in cool-weather environments flourish with blooming heads of broccoli, cauliflower, bok choy, and Brussels sprouts, we're "green" with envy!

Our growing success comes largely in humble bunches of kale, radishes, turnips, and mustard greens. A handful of these seeds will sprout like a swarm of bees on the soil. Radishes, especially, are a joy to grow because of gorgeous varieties like French Breakfast, Watermelon, Purple Plum, and Pink Beauty.

We've yet to refuse to eat anything cruciferous, and these vegetables diversify our menu throughout the year. There's never a mundane moment at a meal in which a cruciferous vegetable is involved. Steamed, grilled, barbecued, sautéed, or eaten raw, these are vegetables that can satisfy.

The health benefits are undeniable as well, so eating anything in the cabbage family makes us feel like superheroes. They seem to have it all: fiber, vitamins, and disease-fighting nutrients.

Throughout the year, cruciferous vegetables are available in different forms and we've grown to appreciate anything with green in more ways than we can count. Salads are essential for spring and summer dinners, and during the autumn and winter months we stuff ourselves with cool-weather kale and winter radishes. During those cooler days, we cuddle up to creamed cabbage, warm kale salads, and savory sautéed mustard greens.

Because this group of vegetables is so broad, it's hard to choose a favorite. The variety of bulbs and leaves keeps our hands busy in the kitchen and our palates excited all year long.

roasted broccoli and grilled cheese melt

MAKES 3 TO 4 SANDWICHES

Life would not be complete without a great grilled cheese sandwich. As many of them as we eat, we never get tired of great bread and good cheese. We also love to experiment with different fillings to enhance the grilled cheese experience, but without distracting from the bread and cheese. This is one of our answers, in which we add roasted broccoli for extra flavor and texture. It's an addictive variation on the classic grilled cheese sandwich—kids love it, and it's a great way to get them to eat their greens.

INGREDIENTS

Florets from 1 medium head broccoli (about ½ pound / 225g), chopped small

2 tablespoons olive oil

½ teaspoon kosher or sea salt

¼ teaspoon freshly cracked black pepper

Unsalted butter, softened

6 to 8 slices bread

1 cup (120g) cheddar or good melting cheese, shredded or thinly sliced

DIRECTIONS

1 Preheat the oven to 400°F (205°C).

2 On a sheet pan, mix the broccoli, oil, salt, and pepper. Roast for 8 to 10 minutes, or until the broccoli is evenly roasted but not burnt. Remove from the oven and allow to cool.

3 Heat a skillet over medium-low heat.

4 Spread butter evenly on one side of each slice of bread. Dividing the ingredients evenly, layer cheese on the unbuttered side of half of the bread slices, then add chopped broccoli in the middle and more cheese on top so that the broccoli lies between two layers of cheese. (This keeps the small pieces of broccoli from falling out as the cheese melts.) Top each with another slice of bread, butter side out.

5 "Grill" in the skillet, turning the sandwiches over once, until the cheese melts and the bread is evenly toasted.

spicy roasted cauliflower
with sriracha and sesame

SERVES 4

Roasted cauliflower with Sriracha is simple, unforgettable, and bound to please hot-sauce addicts. If you love spice and cauliflower, then this Asian-inspired vegetable side dish will bring you the same joy that it's brought us. It's also a crowd pleaser. No doubt the platter will be empty in a matter of minutes, so we suggest doubling or tripling the recipe for a party. Also, anyone who appreciates cauliflower and hot sauce can make a full meal out of this crazy-good vegetable.

INGREDIENTS

⅓ cup (80ml) olive oil

1 teaspoon sesame oil

¾ tablespoon soy sauce

1 tablespoon rice vinegar

2 tablespoons Homemade Sriracha (page 196), or to taste

1 head cauliflower (about 2 pounds / 910g), cut into ¾-inch (2-cm) florets

Minced cilantro, for garnish

DIRECTIONS

1 Preheat the oven to 400°F (205°C). Lightly grease a sheet pan or line it with parchment paper.

2 In a large bowl, combine the oil, sesame oil, soy sauce, vinegar, and Sriracha. Whisk well.

3 Gently add the cauliflower to the bowl and coat with the marinade.

4 Arrange the cauliflower on a baking sheet and roast for 10 minutes. Turn the cauliflower over and roast for another 10 minutes, or until tender.

5 Garnish with the cilantro and serve.

SMASHED CAULIFLOWER SANDWICHES
WITH ROASTED ASPARAGUS PAGE 121

vietnamese napa cabbage chicken salad

SERVES 4 TO 6

From Diane My mother is a wonderful cook, and though I enjoy everything she makes with love in her kitchen, my favorite would have to be her chicken salad. I love everything about this dish, from the fresh herbs to her wonderful fish sauce dressing (though as an adult, I've made a few changes to make it reflect my own personal taste and style—sorry, Mom!) I love using Napa cabbage for its soft and tender texture, but you can certainly use whatever variety of cabbage you like.

INGREDIENTS

2 pounds (910g) boneless, skinless chicken

FOR THE MARINADE

1 tablespoon crushed or grated fresh ginger

2 cloves garlic, crushed

2 tablespoons vegetable oil

2 tablespoons fish sauce

½ teaspoon sugar

FOR THE FISH SAUCE DRESSING

¼ cup (60ml) fish sauce

1 teaspoon grated fresh ginger

3 cloves garlic, minced

1 red chile, minced

1 teaspoon sugar

1 tablespoon fresh lime juice

2 teaspoons rice wine vinegar

6 cups (420g) thinly shredded cabbage (regular or Napa)

1 cup chopped mixed fresh herbs: *rau ram* (Vietnamese coriander), mint, basil, or cilantro

¼ cup (27g) shredded carrots

Crushed roasted peanuts

DIRECTIONS

1 **Make the chicken:** In a large bowl, combine all the chicken marinade ingredients. If your pieces of chicken are thick, place them between two sheets of plastic wrap and pound them with a meat mallet to an even ½-inch (12-mm) thickness. Remove the plastic wrap and add the chicken to the marinade. Let it marinate for 20 minutes.

2 Heat a grill or heavy-bottomed skillet over medium-high heat. Cook the chicken until it is browned and cooked through, 3 to 4 minutes per side. Let cool, then shred or chop the chicken.

3 **Make the fish sauce dressing:** In a medium bowl or large jar, combine all the dressing ingredients with ¾ cup (180ml) water and mix well. Allow the sugar to completely dissolve before using. (You can store the dressing in the refrigerator for up to 1 month.)

4 In a large bowl, combine the cabbage, herbs, and carrots.

5 Add the chicken to the bowl with the cabbage and toss to combine. Add dressing to taste before serving.

6 Top the salad with the peanuts and serve.

warm kale salad
with apples and dried cranberries

SERVES 2 TO 4

Oh, our love of kale can't be topped. We always look forward to growing kale because the different varieties of leaves are gorgeous accents to the garden. After a hearty rain, the raindrops settle and glisten on the leaves like little balls of light. Kale's texture and flavor make salads so interesting and delicious, in both hot and cold applications. This warm, spiced salad variation is perfect for the holiday table, where we often crave something green and healthy. This way, we can eat more pumpkin pie during the holiday meal and not feel so guilty.

INGREDIENTS

2 tablespoons unsalted butter

1 large apple, chopped

⅓ cup (40g) dried cranberries

¼ teaspoon cinnamon

¼ teaspoon kosher or sea salt

1 bunch kale (about ½ pound / 225g), ribs and tough stems removed, leaves chopped

DIRECTIONS

1 In a large sauté pan over medium heat, melt the butter. Once the butter has melted, add the apple, cranberries, cinnamon, and salt.

2 Sauté until the apples are soft, stirring frequently, about 8 minutes.

3 Add the kale and cook until it becomes tender. Serve warm or chilled.

chopped kale salad
massaged with avocado

"Massage" a salad? We were thinking the exact same thing when we first heard it.

During one of our potluck dinner parties, our friend Anne Lee from the dojo contributed this kale salad massaged with avocado. We were blown away by its wonderful flavor, and the "massaged" part was extra-intriguing. She told us she had been inspired by her best friend's recipe and that massaging mashed avocado into the kale leaves makes them softer and more tender.

Giving a delicate rub and some loving avocado touch to the leaves makes them very easy to eat, and the flavor of the avocado still comes through. To season the salad, all you need is a nice squeeze of fresh lemon juice and a little salt and pepper. After that, you can customize your toppings to make this massaged salad completely your own.

INGREDIENTS

1 bunch kale (about ½ pound / 225g), ribs and tough stems removed

2 avocados: 1 mashed, 1 chopped

Fresh lemon juice

Zest of 1 lemon

Kosher or sea salt and freshly cracked pepper

1 small cucumber, chopped

¼ cup (23g) toasted sliced almonds

DIRECTIONS

1 Cut the kale leaves into thin strips. In a large bowl, combine the kale and the mashed avocado. Gently "massage" the avocado into the kale leaves until they become soft and tender.

2 Add 1 tablespoon of lemon juice and the lemon zest. Toss lightly.

3 Season to taste with salt and pepper. Add additional lemon juice, if desired.

4 Just before serving, add the chopped cucumber, the chopped avocado, and the almonds.

kale and chicken egg rolls
with ginger soy dip

MAKES ABOUT 2 DOZEN ROLLS

Another kale recipe? But of course! For those who can't get enough of it (like us!), these egg rolls are another way to indulge in this popular green. The flavor of the kale in these rolls is prominent and satisfying, with the chicken as a secondary element to bind the filling together. Though we often make traditional Vietnamese egg rolls with pork, these kale egg rolls are a more wholesome alternative.

INGREDIENTS

1½ pounds (680g) ground chicken

½ pound (225g) kale, ribs and tough stems removed, leaves chopped into ½-inch (12-mm) pieces

1 egg

½ teaspoon sugar

2 teaspoons fish sauce or soy sauce

2 cloves garlic, finely minced

About 2 dozen 7- to 8-inch (17.5- to 20-cm) egg roll wrappers

Egg white, for sealing wrappers

Vegetable oil, for frying

½ cup (120ml) soy sauce

2 teaspoons grated fresh ginger root

NOTE Most American grocery stores carry thicker, more flour-based wrappers. These fry up to a nice bubbly roll, but take longer to cook, so take this into account when you're frying. At Asian specialty markets, you'll find a greater variety of wrappers, many of which are thinner. These wrappers fry up much lighter and crisper. Select the type that works best for you and, again, take this into account when adjusting frying times.

DIRECTIONS

1 In a medium bowl, combine the chicken, kale, egg, sugar, soy sauce, and garlic. Mix well. Set aside to marinate for 20 to 30 minutes.

2 To roll the egg rolls, place one wrapper at a time on your work surface and spoon about 1 tablespoon of the filling onto the lower one-third of the wrapper. Begin rolling from the bottom, tucking the filling under and folding in the sides as you roll. Brush the edges of the wrapper with egg white to seal them. Set the finished rolls aside on a sheet pan as you finish them.

3 In a large frying pan, heat approximately ¾ inch (2 cm) oil over medium heat. Test the heat of the oil by adding a small piece of egg roll wrapper to the pan. If it sizzles and browns too quickly, then your heat is too high.

4 Gently place the egg rolls in the heated oil and fry for 5 to 10 minutes, or until they are golden on the bottom. Turn the egg rolls over and cook until they are golden on the other side and the filling is cooked through.

5 In a small bowl, combine the soy sauce and ginger and stir well.

6 Serve the egg rolls warm, with the dip on the side.

wilted mizuna mustard salad with shrimp

SERVES 4

Our love of *mizuna* (Japanese mustard greens) came about quite by accident. We were looking at some seed packets at our local gardening store and came across *mizuna* seeds. The image of the mustard plant was so beautiful that we wanted to add it to our garden roster. About two months after seeding, this gorgeous patch of greens proved to be a favorite section of our spring garden. *Mizuna's* mildly spiced and delicately peppery leaves are exciting in salads, especially as a refreshing change from arugula. Adding some grilled shrimp and a fish sauce dressing makes this Asian-inspired salad perfectly balanced and full of flavor.

INGREDIENTS

1 tablespoon unsalted butter

1 tablespoon vegetable oil

2 cloves garlic, crushed

½ pound (225g) shrimp, shelled and deveined

Freshly cracked black pepper

Sea salt

1 large bunch *mizuna* greens or mustard greens, tough stems removed, leaves torn into bite-size pieces

Fish Sauce Dressing (page 124)

DIRECTIONS

1 Heat a pan over medium-high heat, then add the oil, butter, and garlic. Cook for 30 seconds. Add the shrimp and quickly cook until tender, about 30 seconds on each side. Season with pepper and salt to taste.

2 Remove the pan from the heat and add the *mizuna* to the pan. Stir until the *mizuna* is wilted, about 30 seconds. Toss with the fish sauce dressing and serve.

arugula
with braised pork shoulder

SERVES 6 TO 8

From Todd There isn't a leafy green I love more than arugula. In our garden, it is one of the plants that keeps reseeding itself once it has gotten established—so long as we don't pull out the older plants too early. In the kitchen, its peppery kick makes it usable as both an herb and a leafy green. For some people, the larger leaves may have a little too much flavor, but we love its body, heart, and soul. For an additional layer of crunch and flavor, serve some of your favorite pickled vegetables alongside. If you want a tamer version of this recipe, choose baby arugula or replace a bit of the arugula with some regular lettuce instead. The warm pork shoulder contrasting with the cool arugula makes a great winter-weather dish. Keep the pot of pork shoulder warmed nearby for refills throughout the dinner.

INGREDIENTS

- 3 pounds (1.4kg) pork shoulder, cut into ¾-inch (1.5-cm) cubes
- 3-inch (7.5-cm) piece of fresh ginger root, peeled and cut into thin coins
- 10 cloves garlic
- ¾ cup (180ml) dry Marsala wine
- ¾ cup (180ml) sake
- ½ cup (120ml) soy sauce
- ⅓ cup (65g) sugar or ½ cup (75g) palm sugar
- 2 pounds (910g) arugula

DIRECTIONS

1 Place the pork cubes in a large pot and add water to cover the pork by at least 1 inch (2.5 cm). Bring to a boil and continue to boil vigorously for 10 minutes. Strain and rinse the pork. Set aside.

2 In a large clean pot, add the pork, ginger, garlic, 2 cups (480ml) water, the Marsala, sake, soy sauce, and sugar. Bring to a simmer over medium heat, then reduce the heat to low. Simmer, covered but with the lid slightly ajar, stirring occasionally and skimming any foam off the top if needed, for 1½ to 2 hours, or until the pork is tender.

3 Serve the pork warm, topped with arugula. Spoon a bit of the braising liquid over the top as a dressing.

roots & bulbs

NESTLED IN THE EARTH, ROOTS AND BULBS are the most humble of vegetables. They tend to be simple and unassuming. Some of them are better known for their ugliness than their beauty. And most people are unaware of the foliage from many of these rough gems until they actually grow them.

Yet root vegetables are satisfying. Comforting. They are a mother's hug rather than a lover's passionate embrace. Our reactions to them are less dramatic, yet oftentimes much deeper. They warm our souls and make us feel everything will be right in the world.

As photographers, we've stepped out into a farmer's sea of green leaves and found that burrowed beneath them was a trove of sweet potatoes. We watched and photographed his young kids chasing butterflies through leaves reaching up to their waists. Little did they know that a bounty of Thanksgiving treasure lay hidden under their toes.

From our own garden, several roots and bulbs tend to overfill our pantry seasonally. We adore fennel bulbs, but after the first season they started sprouting up in overabundance all over the garden.

(Fortunately the swallowtail butterfly caterpillars love them, so we've benefited from an increase in the local butterfly population.) And hidden beneath their leaves, our beets will quietly grow to monstrous proportions if we don't keep vigilant watch. One particular beet, which we fondly named Henry, grew to nearly ten pounds before we finally pulled him up.

But even in their overgrown state, these hearty vegetables can still be salvaged. Beets are wonderful when prepared in the right fashion. Don't attempt to whittle them down and roast the chunks for a delicate beet salad. Instead, slice them thin and bake them into chips for an addictive snack.

These wonderful roots and bulbs, which nourish and comfort us, seem to gracefully handle our callous neglect. Yet despite such durability, we cannot let ourselves forget how good they can be when handled with the joy and care so many of our other fruits and vegetables get. The sweet creaminess of a freshly picked fingerling potato or the brilliant flavor of a finely shaved fennel bulb in its plump prime—these are glorious tastes to experience.

olive oil–baked beet chips
with sea salt and black pepper

SERVES 2 TO 4

The sweet, earthy root flavor of beet chips is a nice change from the classic potato chip. Invest a little time and effort in making these chips and you'll have a new favorite snack. Their crunch will vary depending on how thickly you slice the beet root and how much oil you use. We highly recommend using a mandoline to keep the slices thin and consistent. When the raw beet slices are baked, they will shrink considerably, so use large roots. To avoid staining your hands, wear plastic gloves when slicing and handling the beets.

INGREDIENTS

2 pounds (910g) large beets
2 tablespoons olive oil
¼ teaspoon sea salt
Freshly cracked black pepper

DIRECTIONS

1 Preheat the oven to 350°F (175°C). Line several sheet pans with parchment paper.

2 Wearing gloves to prevent staining your hands, peel the beets.

3 Using a mandoline, thinly slice the beets to a thickness of 1/16 inch (1.5 mm).

4 In a large bowl, combine the beet slices and oil. Rub the oil evenly over the slices.

5 On the prepared sheet pans, in a single layer, arrange as many slices as will fit without crowding. Bake until crisp, 25 to 30 minutes, rotating the pans once halfway through baking.

6 Cool the chips and blot them on paper towels to remove any excess oil.

7 Repeat steps 5 and 6, using a cool sheet pan lined with parchment paper for each batch, until all the beet slices are baked.

8 Toss the chips in a large bowl with the salt and pepper to taste.

seared ginger carrots
with thyme and shallots

SERVES 4

This is a quick alternative to classic glazed carrots. Everything is cooked over high heat for a brief moment, so you'll want to make sure you have everything prepped before starting to cook. Because of the high heat, make sure to use oil with a high flash point, such as grapeseed, peanut, or canola oil. Don't use that precious olive oil for this recipe.

INGREDIENTS

1 tablespoon grapeseed oil
(or other high-flash-point oil)

1 tablespoon unsalted butter

¾ pound (340g) carrots, sliced
¼ inch (6 mm) thick

¼ pound (115g) shallots, peeled
and sliced into rings

1 tablespoon crushed or minced
garlic (from about 3 cloves)

1 inch (2.5 cm) fresh ginger root,
peeled and grated or finely
diced

1 teaspoon chopped fresh thyme
leaves

2 teaspoons sugar

1 teaspoon kosher or sea salt

½ teaspoon fresh lemon juice

DIRECTIONS

1 Heat a sauté pan over high heat. Add the oil and butter, then quickly add the carrots. Cook for 2 minutes, stirring a couple times.

2 Add the shallots, garlic, ginger, thyme, sugar, and salt. Cook for 2 more minutes, or until the shallots are soft and the carrots are just tender.

3 Stir in the lemon juice, remove from the heat, and serve.

roasted parsley root
with red quinoa

SERVES 4

Often mistaken for parsnip, parsley root has flavors of both carrot and parsley. The unique taste of parsley root brings a wonderful element of interest to many classic whole-grain salads. This simple roasted preparation of roasted parsley root and red quinoa is a satisfying meal in itself.

INGREDIENTS

1 pound (455g) parsley roots, cleaned and halved

1 tablespoon olive oil

Kosher or sea salt, to taste

Freshly cracked black pepper, to taste

1 cup (170g) red quinoa

FOR THE DRESSING

3 tablespoons olive oil

1½ tablespoons fresh lemon juice

½ teaspoon Worcestershire sauce

⅓ teaspoon Dijon mustard

1 tablespoon finely chopped fresh flat-leaf parsley (or parsley root tops if you have them)

½ teaspoon kosher or sea salt

1 teaspoon sugar

Sprigs of fresh parsley, for garnish

DIRECTIONS

1 Preheat the oven to 400°F (205°C).

2 On a sheet pan, combine the parsley root and oil. Spread the parsley root halves in a single layer. Season with salt and pepper. Roast for 15 to 20 minutes, until tender.

3 In a saucepan, combine the quinoa with 2 cups (480ml) water. Bring to a simmer, cover, then reduce the heat to low and cook for 15 minutes, or until the water is fully absorbed.

4 **Make the dressing:** In a bowl, whisk together the dressing ingredients.

5 In a medium bowl, toss the quinoa with the dressing. Plate the quinoa and top with the roasted parsley roots. Garnish with a sprig of parsley.

hearty celery root and red lentil soup

SERVES 4 TO 6

Soup is a staple in our way of eating. Bowls of brothy comfort make an appearance at the table at least a few times a week. We're even crazy enough to eat soup on hot summer days. But it's during the chilly months of fall and winter that it's most satisfying to have soup on a daily basis. One-pot soup meals—studded with chunks of celery root, salted with bacon, fragranced with sage, and laced with red lentils—are all we need to welcome the cold days. If you've never had celery root before, we encourage you to try it. It has the texture of a potato, with the bright flavor of fresh, green celery.

INGREDIENTS

1 medium celery root (about 1 pound / 455g)

4 slices thick-cut bacon, sliced into small pieces

1 medium onion, minced

5 cloves garlic, minced

1 (2-inch / 5-cm) knob fresh ginger, peeled and crushed whole

2 to 3 small sage leaves

¼ cup (50g) red lentils

Sea salt

DIRECTIONS

1 Cut the celery root into bite-size pieces.

2 Heat a medium pot over medium heat, add the bacon, and cook until the fat is rendered. Add the onion, garlic, ginger, and sage leaves. Cook for 5 minutes, or until the onions are translucent.

3 Add 4 cups (960ml) water and the celery root, bring to a simmer, then reduce the heat to low.

4 Cook for 15 minutes, or until the celery root is almost tender. Add the lentils and cook until they are soft (see Note) and the celery root is cooked through. Taste for seasoning and add salt if necessary. Serve hot.

NOTE Cook the lentils to your desired texture. Some cooks prefer lentils still whole and firm rather than soft and mushy.

potatoes au gratin

SERVES 6 TO 8

From Todd This is an all-time favorite cold-weather dish. If I were given the chance to choose the dishes for my final feast, these potatoes would be among them. The beauty is in the simplicity of technique. There is no cheese—just cream, which is allowed to slowly cook its way into the potatoes, gently breaking down and helping to form a final crust. To keep the cream from burning, you'll break the crust with the back of a spoon every twenty to thirty minutes, allowing a fresh layer to makes its way to the top. Then in the final half hour, the top is left untouched, allowing it to bake into a beautiful golden cover.

If you are making a large batch, put the peeled potatoes in a bowl of water to keep them from browning. This is also a great opportunity to hone your knife skills, but for an alternative method, slice with a mandoline or food processor slicing blade. Personally I prefer slicing by hand; it's a bit meditative, with the added challenge of playing with a sharp knife.

INGREDIENTS	DIRECTIONS
2 cloves garlic	1 Preheat the oven to 350°F (175°C).
4 pounds (1.8kg) potatoes	2 Crack the garlic cloves to break them up slightly, then use them to rub the insides of a 2-quart (2-L) baking dish. Set the dish aside.
1 tablespoon kosher or sea salt	
2 teaspoons freshly cracked black pepper	
½ teaspoon freshly grated nutmeg	3 Peel and slice the potatoes ⅛ inch (3 mm) thick.
2½ cups (600ml) heavy cream	4 Put the sliced potatoes into a large bowl and season with the salt, pepper, and nutmeg. Get your hands in there and toss well to coat the slices evenly. Slap a potato slice against your tongue to test for seasoning. It should be noticeably seasoned but not overpowering so.
	5 Layer the potatoes into the prepared dish, smoothing the tops so they are fairly level. Pour the cream over the potatoes to the point where you can press down on the top layer and the potato slices disappear under the cream. Press the slices down a couple of times, then taste the cream for seasoning. Add a sprinkle of salt, if needed.

recipe continues

6 Bake for a total of 1½ to 2 hours (larger batches will take longer than smaller ones). Every 30 minutes or so, open the oven and, using the back of a large spoon, break the crust the cream is starting to form. On the final crust-breaking, the consistency of the cream should be noticeably thicker and it should have been fairly well absorbed into the potatoes. For the final 30 minutes of baking, leave everything untouched, in order to form a crisp golden top. The cream should be almost fully absorbed, leaving just a bit of creamy butteriness between the potato slices.

7 Remove from the oven and allow to cool slightly before serving. The potatoes will retain an intense heat for at least 15 minutes.

herb-smashed turnips
with parmesan

SERVES 4 TO 6

When we're hungry for the texture of mashed potatoes yet craving something lighter, we turn to these herb-smashed turnips. Root vegetables are always so versatile and turnips are no exception. Fresh herbs brighten up the turnips and some Parmesan adds a nice touch of richness and tang. When we grow them, an extra-special treat is having big baskets full of tender turnip greens to add to salads so that no parts of the turnips are wasted.

INGREDIENTS

2 large turnips (about 2 pounds / 910g), peeled and cut into 1-inch (2.5-cm) cubes

1 bay leaf

2 tablespoons milk

Kosher or sea salt

Freshly cracked black pepper

½ to 1 teaspoon chopped fresh herbs, such as rosemary, thyme, parsley, or mint

½ cup (50g) freshly grated Parmesan

1 tablespoon chopped fresh chives

DIRECTIONS

1 Place the turnips in a large pot. Fill the pot with water to cover, add the bay leaf, and bring to a boil.

2 Boil the turnips for 20 to 30 minutes, or until soft. Drain the turnips well, then transfer to a large bowl.

3 In a separate bowl, combine the milk, 1 teaspoon salt, pepper to taste, the herbs, and the Parmesan. Add the mixture to the turnips and smash to your desired texture. (We prefer them on the chunky side, but you can also puree them in a food processor to a smooth, creamy texture.)

4 Taste and season with more salt, if desired. Garnish with the chives and serve warm.

pizza dough

MAKES TWO 10-INCH PIZZAS

Over the years we've loved studying and learning about bread—especially pizzas. It is something of an obsession of ours to try and find the best wood-fired pizza in each city we travel to. We've learned a lot from listening to great bakers and watching them bake their doughs. One thing they all seem to have in common is that they don't overhandle the dough. The more you work it, the tougher it gets. With most of the great pizzas we've had, the bakers are not kneading their dough, but just mixing it and letting the yeast go to work. And when they handle their dough to make pizzas, it isn't with a heavy, forceful hand, but rather by gently letting gravity stretch and form the dough. It is graceful and gentle. The amount of flour in the recipe should yield a dough that will be easy to handle with just a touch of extra flour for dusting when you are stretching it. If you are comfortable with handling the dough, experiment with putting a bit less flour in it. This will make for a lighter crust, but because the dough is wetter, it will be a bit more challenging to work with.

INGREDIENTS

1¼ cups (300ml) warm water

1 teaspoon active dry yeast

1 teaspoon honey

1½ teaspoons kosher or sea salt

3⅓ cups (415g) flour

DIRECTIONS

1 In a large bowl or resealable container, stir together the water, yeast, honey, and salt. Stir in the flour until no streak of flour remains.

2 Cover the dough and set aside in a warm area to proof for 1 to 2 hours, or until doubled in volume. Set aside in the refrigerator until chilled, or for up to 1 week (see Note).

3 When you are ready to make pizzas, divide the dough in half and place the dough balls on a well-floured surface. Allow the dough to come to room temperature for about 30 minutes. The dough should feel soft and pillowy.

4 With floured hands, lightly flour the first dough ball. Using your hands, rotate and gently pull out the dough, working from the center outward to stretch it, leaving the outer rim as untouched as possible. Stretch to a circle 7 to 8 inches (17.5 to 20 cm) in diameter.

5 Resting the dough on the tops of your hands, continue to rotate and circle, gently stretching the dough to about 10 inches (25 cm) in diameter. Make sure to keep the rim thicker than the center. (If the dough starts to toughen and spring back too much while you work on it, allow it to rest for a few minutes so it will relax and soften.) Lightly re-flour your hands, the work surface, and the dough as needed to keep the dough from sticking.

6 Use the dough as directed in individual recipes, such as those on pages 153 and 154.

NOTE Over time in the fridge, the dough will gradually begin to change in texture after it bakes, and will also develop a sourdough flavor. We prefer the texture and flavor of the dough after 24 to 36 hours of refrigeration, but it is still quite good when chilled up to 1 week.

PIZZA WITH ROSEMARY POTATOES PAGE 153
PIZZA WITH CARAMELIZED FENNEL, ARUGULA, AND LEMON PAGE 154

pizza with rosemary potatoes

MAKES 2 PIZZAS

Anytime we have a potato pizza it takes us back to our first trip to Italy. It was there, on the streets of Rome, that we were first introduced to pizza and potato married together. It has been a favorite ever since. A word of warning, though: The potato slices baked with rosemary are highly addictive, so you might want to make extra for snacking on. Somehow half of the tray seems to disappear before the pizzas are ever assembled.

INGREDIENTS

1 pound (455g) fingerling or other baby potatoes, sliced ¼ inch (6 mm) thick

1 tablespoon finely chopped fresh rosemary

1 teaspoon kosher or sea salt

2 tablespoons olive oil, plus more for brushing crust

1 batch Pizza Dough (page 148)

½ cup (120ml) Homemade Barbecue Sauce (page 56) or tomato sauce

½ cup (65g) grated smoked Gouda or other preferred cheese

NOTE A peel is a wooden, shovel-shaped tool used to slide pizzas into and out of the oven.

DIRECTIONS

1 Preheat the oven to 425°F (220°C). Line a sheet pan with parchment paper.

2 Combine the potato slices, rosemary, salt, and oil on the lined sheet pan. Toss to evenly coat the potatoes.

3 Bake for 15 minutes, or until the potatoes are light golden. Set aside.

4 Place a baking stone on the middle rack of your oven and raise the oven temperature to 550°F (290°C), or as hot as your oven will go.

5 Divide the pizza dough in two and stretch the first half. (See instructions in the Pizza Dough recipe, page 148.) Brush the edges of the dough with oil. Place the dough on a floured peel (see Note) and shake the dough on the peel to make sure it isn't sticking.

6 Spread the sauce evenly over the pizza. Add half of the potatoes, then sprinkle with the cheese. Bake for 10 minutes, or until the crust is golden.

7 While the first pizza bakes, repeat the procedure in step 5 with the second dough half. After the first pizza is out of the oven, repeat step 6 with the second pizza.

8 Slice and serve.

pizza with caramelized fennel, arugula, and lemon

MAKES 2 PIZZAS

The fragrance of freshly shaved fennel bulb is perfume to the kitchen. Its sweet licorice aroma and delicate grassy notes also make it a perfect topping for a vegetarian pizza. We become so excited for the fennel bulbs that grow year after year. It would be great to be able to take credit for them, but the wind and Mother Nature are the real forces behind the fresh fennel that feeds us each year. But we can at least take credit for this pizza that we love eating so much!

INGREDIENTS

Olive oil

2 cloves garlic, crushed

1 fennel bulb, thinly sliced

1 batch Pizza Dough (page 148)

About 1 pound (455g) heirloom tomatoes, sliced ¼ inch (6 mm) thick

Sea salt

Freshly cracked black pepper

½ cup (50g) freshly grated Parmesan

Finely grated zest of 1 lemon

1 cup (20g) baby arugula

DIRECTIONS

1 Place a baking stone on the middle rack of your oven and preheat the oven to 550°F (290°C), or as hot as your oven will go.

2 In a bowl, combine 2 tablespoons oil, the garlic, and the fennel.

3 Divide the pizza dough in two and stretch the first half. (See instructions in Pizza Dough recipe, page 148.) Brush the edges of the dough with oil. Place the dough on a floured peel (see Note, page 153) and shake the dough on the peel to make sure it isn't sticking.

4 Layer the tomato slices onto the pizza. Sprinkle with ½ teaspoon sea salt and pepper to taste. Pick the fennel out of the bowl and layer it on the pizza. Sprinkle with about one-third of the Parmesan. Bake for 10 minutes, or until the crust is golden.

5 While the first pizza bakes, repeat step 3 with the second dough half. After the first pizza is out of the oven, repeat step 4 with the second pizza.

6 Sprinkle the lemon zest over the pizzas. Slice. Top evenly with the arugula and the remaining Parmesan. If you wish, drizzle a little olive oil and sprinkle a dash of sea salt over the arugula.

jicama chicken cashew salad
with mustard dressing

SERVES 4 TO 6

Jicama root doesn't get enough love. It's a perfect alternative to carrots or celery, and adding it to this party salad results in the perfect crunch and texture. We can easily eat a whole jicama by ourselves as a snack, and to make it extra indulgent, we'll dip it in ranch dressing. Yes, we're often guilty of dipping fresh veggies in ranch dressing. You only live once.

INGREDIENTS

FOR THE CHICKEN

2 tablespoons vegetable oil

1 small onion, minced

2 cloves garlic, minced

1 pound (455g) chicken breast cutlets, cut into ½-inch (12-mm) cubes

1 tablespoon grated fresh ginger

1 teaspoon soy sauce

Freshly cracked black pepper

FOR THE DRESSING

½ cup (120 ml) mayonnaise

2 teaspoons Dijon mustard

¼ teaspoon kosher salt

¼ teaspoon freshly cracked black pepper

1 teaspoon apple cider vinegar

FOR THE SALAD

1 small jicama root (about 2 pounds / 910g), peeled and cut into strips

½ cup (50g) chopped celery

½ cup (45g) roasted cashews

3 scallions, sliced thin

DIRECTIONS

1 **Make the chicken:** In a large pan, heat the oil over medium heat. Add the onion and garlic and cook until soft.

2 Raise the heat to medium-high. Add the chicken, ginger, soy sauce, and pepper to taste and cook the chicken, stirring occasionally, until it is lightly browned and cooked through, about 6 minutes. Allow to cool.

3 **Make the dressing:** In a bowl, whisk together all the dressing ingredients.

4 **Assemble the salad:** In a large bowl, combine the cooked chicken, jicama, celery, cashews, scallions, and the dressing. Toss together well; allow to chill for about 1 hour before serving.

sweet potato and chocolate squares

MAKES 12 SQUARES

We enjoy a good sweet potato pie, but oftentimes it's consumed after a huge holiday feast, when our bellies are bursting with turkey and stuffing. So we have transformed this special dessert into small squares so that we can slowly savor the deliciousness one bite at a time. Chocolate has been added to these squares too, and we think you'll agree that sweet potato and chocolate make a killer pairing!

INGREDIENTS

FOR THE CRUST

¾ cup (110g) graham cracker crumbs (from about 9 whole graham crackers)

½ cup (50g) finely ground pecans or other nuts

1 teaspoon finely grated fresh ginger root

¼ cup (55g) packed brown sugar

¼ teaspoon kosher or sea salt

5 tablespoons (70g) unsalted butter, melted

½ teaspoon vanilla extract

FOR THE CHOCOLATE FILLING

⅓ cup (80ml) heavy cream

¼ pound (115g) dark chocolate, cut into small pieces

FOR THE SWEET POTATO FILLING

1 cup sweet potato puree (opposite)

2 large eggs, slightly beaten

½ teaspoon kosher or sea salt

1 teaspoon ground cinnamon

Pinch ground cloves

ingredients continue

DIRECTIONS

1 Preheat the oven to 350°F (175°C).

2 **Make the crust:** In a bowl, combine the crust ingredients and mix thoroughly. Press the mixture into a 9-by-9-inch (22.5-by-22.5-cm) square baking dish or pan, pressing the crust 1 inch (2.5 cm) up the sides. Bake for 15 minutes. Remove from the oven and set aside to cool. Keep the oven heated.

3 **Make the chocolate filling:** In a saucepan, combine the cream and chocolate. Cook over low heat, stirring frequently, until the chocolate is melted and completely combined with the cream. Pour the mixture over the crust; tilt and gently shake the pan to spread the mixture evenly. Set aside to cool for at least 10 minutes before adding the sweet potato filling.

4 **Make the sweet potato filling:** In a bowl, combine the sweet potato filling ingredients and mix well.

5 Gently pour the sweet potato filling over the chocolate layer. Place the baking dish on the middle rack of the oven. Bake for 40 to 50 minutes, or until the outer inch appears set; the center should still wiggle slightly when shaken. Set aside to cool, then refrigerate until fully chilled.

6 Slice with a clean knife into even squares, wiping the knife clean before each cut.

¼ cup (55g) packed brown sugar

¼ cup (50g) granulated sugar

1 cup (240ml) milk

½ cup (120ml) heavy cream

FOR THE TOPPING
(OPTIONAL)

1 cup (240ml) heavy cream

1 teaspoon confectioners' sugar

½ teaspoon vanilla extract

Pecan halves, for garnish

7 **Make the topping (optional):** In a bowl, whip together the cream, confectioners' sugar, and vanilla extract until soft peaks form. Garnish the squares with the whipped cream and pecans, if you like.

SWEET POTATO PUREE

MAKES 1 CUP

To make sweet potato puree, prepare the sweet potatoes in one of these two ways:

Bake 1 pound (455g) of sweet potatoes, with skins on, at 375°F (190°C) until soft, about 1½ hours. Cool the potatoes slightly, peel, and press through a fine-mesh sieve. Or, peel the potatoes and boil them until soft, 20 to 30 minutes, then press through a fine-mesh sieve. Baking is slightly more flavorful, but boiling is much quicker.

sweet onion crack dip

SERVES 4 TO 6

Our friends and guests dubbed this warm cheesy dip the "crack dip." It's a guilty pleasure that everyone is addicted to, regardless of how full they are. They can't stop eating it until the bowl is swiped empty with the last piece of bread. Part of what makes this crack dip extra-special is baking it until a charred brown crust forms on top; this brings out the smoky flavor of all the melted cheese and sweet onion. Once you try it, you'll know why it's our number-one party dip!

INGREDIENTS

1 (8-ounce / 225-g) package cream cheese (very softened)

1 cup (240ml) mayonnaise (preferably Best Foods brand)

1 cup (100g) freshly grated Parmesan

1 cup (160g) diced sweet onion

1 tablespoon freshly cracked black pepper

Crusty bread or crackers

DIRECTIONS

1 Preheat the oven to 350°F (175°C).

2 In a bowl, place the cream cheese. The cream cheese must be very soft (like spreadable butter) to allow all the ingredients to blend evenly. If your cream cheese needs to soften more, place it in the microwave for a few seconds.

3 Add the mayonnaise, Parmesan, onion, and pepper and mix until everything is thoroughly combined.

4 Pour the mixture into a 6-inch (15-cm) baking dish or any oven-safe dish. Bake for 40 to 50 minutes, so all the ingredients meld together. When the top crust is brown and almost burnt-looking, the dip is ready. The darker brown the crust becomes, the better the flavors are.

5 Serve with your favorite crusty bread or crackers.

squashes

AUTUMN USUALLY COMES TO MIND FIRST when we think of squash, yet these vegetable-fruits are a part of our table for more than half the year.

The warm weather brings us the summer squashes to fill our garden: zucchinis, patty pans, and yellow crooknecks. Their massive leaves protect the soil from weed invasion. Their flowers become an edible treat or a beautiful landing pad for bumblebees. The fruit of these utilitarian garden cornerstones are a curiosity of their own. It is a bit peculiar to think of something as being "perfectly ripe" when it is immature, yet that is the case with summer squash. The zucchinis are firm, not spongy. Their rinds are tender and the squash are perfect to bring into the kitchen.

That window of ripeness is short during the long days of summer, however. We always intend to pick the squash when we should, but summer is filled with play and travel, and all too often those perfect tender zucchini swell to comical proportions during a few days' absence. Fortunately, for every one lost to the compost pile, there are several others quickly taking its place.

As the weather changes to the cool air and crisp dryness of autumn, the summer squashes' brethren take over our dinner tables, as winter squashes and their hearty comfort find a home on our plates. We begin to bundle up when we go outdoors, and in the kitchen we transition from grilling and searing to roasting and basting.

The winter squashes have been growing along their vines all summer. By autumn they are fully mature, their colors are deep and rich, their outer shells have hardened, and they are ready. With our busy holiday schedules, winter squash bring the added bonus of an incredible shelf life. Most will keep for months in a cool spot (not the refrigerator, though) without risk of spoilage.

The variety is tremendous. There is the classic pumpkin, with its relatives: sugar pumpkins, New England Pie pumpkins, and Cinderella pumpkins are all fantastic sources of homemade pumpkin puree. Butternut squash has to be one of our favorite squashes of all time. With its sweet, earthy, and nutty characteristics, the butternut pairs amazingly well with sage and mushrooms. Then there is the cute acorn squash. Resembling oversize nuts, they are perfect for roasting. Roasted in wedges, seasoned with anything from apples and brown butter to your favorite curry, they are an amazing addition to any autumn table. And don't be lulled into thinking that all squash have the same texture. Spaghetti squash will separate into delicious spaghettilike strands after cooking, and it's great with just about any pasta sauce we've thrown at it.

Fall is the feasting season. What better way to feast than with the diverse bounty of squash?

summer squash stuffed with teriyaki pork

SERVES 6

Every year it's the same: We can't ever keep up with our patch of summer squash. They grow like weeds, and it feels like they've gotten twelve inches larger in forty-eight hours. We've even had fun games on our blog to see if anyone can guess the weight of our largest zucchini. So far, we've topped twenty-five pounds for a single squash. The summer squash in our garden seem to have minds of their own. To keep up with them, we've tried many different variations of stuffed squash, but the most popular version is stuffing them with pork mixed with homemade teriyaki sauce.

INGREDIENTS

3 to 4 medium summer squash or zucchini

1 tablespoon vegetable oil, plus more for brushing

½ small onion, minced

2 cloves garlic, minced

1 teaspoon grated fresh ginger

2 tablespoons chopped fresh flat-leaf parsley

½ pound (225g) ground pork

1 teaspoon fish sauce or soy sauce

2 tablespoons Homemade Teriyaki Sauce (page 292)

¼ cup (25g) bread crumbs

DIRECTIONS

1 Preheat oven to 350°F (175°C).

2 Cut the squash in half lengthwise. Using a small spoon, scoop out the center seeds and scrape out enough space for the pork filling.

3 In a large pan, heat the oil over medium heat. Add the onion, garlic, and ginger, and cook until the onion is crisp but not burnt. Turn off the heat and allow the mixture to cool.

4 Add the parsley and ground pork to the pan with the onion-garlic mixture. Add the fish sauce and the teriyaki sauce and stir to combine.

5 Brush the outsides of the squash with oil. Dividing the pork mixture evenly, stuff it into the squash halves until they are full.

6 Place the squash on a sheet pan and bake, covered with foil, for 15 minutes. Remove the foil, top the pork mixture with the bread crumbs, and bake, uncovered, for 15 minutes more, or until the pork is completely cooked.

curried kabocha squash and chicken stew

SERVES 6

Kabocha squash is often called Japanese pumpkin, and it's beloved for its naturally sweet flavor. Look past its knobby skin to see the gorgeous golden flesh that cooks to a delicate consistency. (The raw flesh is firm and hard, so please be careful when cutting and peeling it.) Our cold winter days are warmed by this kabocha and chicken stew, and the added scent of curry brings comfort to the house. Add a loaf of your favorite crusty bread, and you'll have a complete meal that warms the stomach, the soul, and the house all at the same time.

If you can't find this cute, squat-looking green squash, you can replace it with butternut squash.

INGREDIENTS

2 tablespoons vegetable oil

1 medium onion, minced

3 cloves garlic, minced

2 pounds (910g) boneless, skinless chicken breast, cubed

1 small kabocha squash (about 3 pounds / 1.4kg), peeled, seeded, and cut into ¾-inch (2-cm) chunks

2 tablespoons fish sauce

1 (1-inch / 2.5-cm) knob of ginger, peeled and lightly smashed

1½ tablespoons curry powder

½ cup (120ml) coconut milk

Kosher or sea salt and freshly cracked black pepper

Fresh cilantro and scallions, chopped, for garnish

DIRECTIONS

1 In a large pot, heat the oil over medium heat. Add the onion and garlic and cook until soft.

2 Add the chicken and cook until browned, about 3 minutes.

3 Add the squash, fish sauce, ginger, curry powder, coconut milk, salt and pepper to taste, and 2 cups (480ml) water. Stir to combine.

4 Turn the heat to low and cook for 20 to 30 minutes, or until the squash is tender. If needed, add additional water to cover the squash, about ¼ cup (60ml) at a time. (Season to taste with extra salt and pepper if you add additional water.) Garnish with the cilantro and scallions and serve.

roasted gold nugget squash with apples and brown butter

SERVES 4

Sometimes there's nothing better than a warm roasted-squash dish to kick-start the holiday season. A festive alternative to traditional acorn squash is Gold Nugget squash. These popular winter squash have bright orange skins and look like small pumpkins. Their sweet, buttery flesh roasts to a wonderfully soft texture. Paired with apples, brown sugar, and pecans, this side dish is always a hit at our fall and winter gatherings. If you can't locate Gold Nuggets, acorn squash will work beautifully as well.

INGREDIENTS

3 tablespoons unsalted butter

3 tablespoons brown sugar

½ teaspoon cinnamon

2 medium apples (about ½ pound / 225g total), cored and sliced

1 medium Gold Nugget squash (about 1½ pounds / 680g), peeled, seeded, and sliced ½ inch (12 mm) thick

½ cup (60g) chopped pecans

Sea salt

Freshly cracked black pepper

DIRECTIONS

1 Preheat the oven to 375°F (190°C).

2 In a medium saucepan, melt the butter over medium heat. After the butter stops sizzling, add the brown sugar and cinnamon. Stir until well combined.

3 Add the apples and sauté for 5 minutes, or until the apples are soft.

4 On a sheet pan, toss the squash and the pecans with the apple mixture. Coat completely, then spread out the squash into an even layer in the pan. Season to taste with salt and pepper.

5 Roast for 15 to 20 minutes, or until tender. Serve warm.

zucchini-cardamom mini tea cakes

MAKES 15 MINI CAKES

Rarely do our friends and neighbors turn down a warm loaf of zucchini bread. But lately we've been sharing a unique version of this classic bread by making it into small, bite-size cakes. To add to the fun, we've spiced them with earthy cardamom, turning them into perfect little cakes for tea or coffee. We've used small tartlet molds, but if you want to keep the shape simple, you can use mini muffin pans as well; just remember to lengthen the baking time if the molds are much bigger than two inches wide by one inch deep. And don't forget the nice sprinkle of confectioners' sugar!

INGREDIENTS

Vegetable oil, for the molds

1 cup (125g) flour

1 teaspoon baking powder

¼ teaspoon ground cardamom

½ teaspoon aniseed

Pinch of kosher or sea salt

½ pound (225g) zucchini, grated

1 egg

½ cup (100g) sugar

½ teaspoon finely grated lime zest (about 1 medium lime)

½ cup (1 stick / 113g) unsalted butter, melted

Confectioners' sugar for dusting

DIRECTIONS

1 Preheat the oven to 325°F (165°C). Lightly oil fifteen 2½-inch (6-cm) tartlet molds.

2 In a bowl, whisk together the flour, baking powder, cardamom, aniseed, and salt. Set aside.

3 Squeeze the grated zucchini dry with paper towels or clean kitchen towels.

4 In a separate bowl, whisk together the egg, sugar, and lime zest. Whisk in the butter. Stir in the zucchini. Fold in the flour mixture until just combined.

5 Divide the batter evenly among the tartlet molds, filling each one almost to the top. Place the molds on a sheet pan and bake for 20 to 25 minutes, or until the cakes are light golden and a toothpick inserted in the center comes out clean.

6 Allow the cakes to cool, remove from the molds, and dust with confectioners' sugar before serving.

roasted-pumpkin ice cream

MAKES ABOUT 1½ QUARTS (1.5 L)

It seems as if just a few years ago it was almost impossible to find pie pumpkins, even in October, but now we are seeing them everywhere. Yay! Roasting a pumpkin for puree is one of the most minimal-effort-for-maximum-gain-over-store-bought things you can do in the kitchen. Make sure to use pie pumpkins or sugar pumpkins, not the jack-o'-lantern behemoths—those big boys don't have the best taste or texture. If you are roasting a large heirloom pumpkin, cutting it in half and roasting it on an oiled sheet pan, cut side down, will shorten the cooking time.

INGREDIENTS

1 small pie pumpkin (makes about 2 cups / 480ml puree)

½ teaspoon vanilla extract

1 teaspoon ground cinnamon

½ teaspoon freshly grated nutmeg

⅛ teaspoon ground cloves

¼ cup (55g) packed brown sugar

1 quart (1L) Vanilla Rum Ice Cream (page 262) or store-bought vanilla ice cream (see Note)

NOTE There is a long way and a short way to make this ice cream. Go crazy and make your own vanilla rum ice cream, stirring the puree and spices into the ice cream just after you finish churning. Or for the short version, let a container of your favorite vanilla ice cream soften up, then stir in the pumpkin and spices.

DIRECTIONS

1 Turn the oven to 375°F (190°C); you do not need to preheat.

2 Place the pumpkin on a sheet pan and roast for about 1 hour, until it feels soft when you press its sides. Remove it from the oven and set aside until cool enough to handle.

3 Split the pumpkin open and remove all the seeds and stringy bits, then scrape out the flesh. Puree the flesh in a blender or food processor until smooth.

4 Stir the vanilla extract, cinnamon, nutmeg, cloves, and brown sugar into the puree.

5 Allow the ice cream to soften and stir in the puree. You may either serve the soft ice cream immediately or allow it to harden up in the freezer before serving.

roasted spaghetti squash with sausage

SERVES 4

Spaghetti squash is a perfect substitute for pasta or noodles when you're craving that texture without the heavy starch. There are lots of recipes that call for microwaving spaghetti squash, but we prefer roasting it; this brings out the taste and texture of the squash. If you're pressed for time, you can always roast the spaghetti squash in this recipe ahead of time, then quickly heat it in the pan with the sausage when you need to serve it. Try not to overcook the squash to the point where it becomes soft and mushy; it should still have a bit of a bite.

INGREDIENTS

2 tablespoons olive oil

1 spaghetti squash (about 3 pounds / 1.4kg)

¾ pound (340g) uncooked sausage (any kind)

5 or 6 medium shallots, thickly sliced

3 cloves garlic, crushed or minced

1 cup (100g) coarsely grated Parmigiana Reggiano

1 tablespoon finely chopped fresh oregano, or other herb complementary to the sausage

Kosher or sea salt

Freshly cracked black pepper

NOTE Use the tip of the knife to first pierce the squash and get the cut started. Then the rest of the squash should slice easily.

DIRECTIONS

1 Preheat the oven to 375°C (190°C). Oil a sheet pan with 1 tablespoon of the oil.

2 Slice the squash in half lengthwise (see Note). Scoop out the seeds and stringy bits, then place the squash, cut sides down, on the prepared pan.

3 Bake for 35 to 45 minutes, or until a fork easily separates the squash flesh into strands. Loosen and remove the "spaghetti" from the shells and set aside.

4 Pinch and pull small balls of the sausage out of its casing, arranging them so they stay slightly separate.

5 In a large sauté pan, heat the remaining tablespoon oil over medium heat. Add the shallots and garlic. Cook until soft, stirring, then add the sausage. Cook, untouched, until the sausage starts to brown, then stir. Continue cooking, stirring occasionally, until the sausage is cooked through, 2 to 3 minutes.

6 Add the squash strands to the sausage and continue cooking until heated through, about 1 minute.

7 Remove the pan from the heat. Toss in the Parmigiana Reggiano and oregano. Season with salt and pepper to taste. Serve immediately.

butternut squash crumble

SERVES 8

Inspired by our favorite truffled butternut squash soups, this recipe transforms similar ingredients into an amazing savory crumble. Truffled olive oil really punches up the flavor, but if you can't find any, the recipe is still excellent without it.

INGREDIENTS

Butter, for the baking dish

FOR THE FILLING

2 tablespoons (30ml) olive oil

1 teaspoon truffled olive oil (optional)

3 to 4 large (115g) shallots, thinly sliced

2 cloves garlic, minced

2 ounces bacon or pancetta (about 2 strips), chopped

1 cup (70g) finely chopped brown mushrooms

3 pounds (1.4kg) butternut squash, peeled and cut into ¾-inch (2-cm) pieces

2 tablespoons chopped fresh flat-leaf parsley

1 sage leaf, finely chopped

½ cup (120ml) chicken stock

Salt and freshly cracked black pepper

FOR THE CRUMBLE TOPPING

¾ cup (95g) all-purpose flour

¼ cup (30g) finely chopped walnuts

1 tablespoon brown sugar

1 tablespoon chopped fresh thyme

1 teaspoon salt

Freshly cracked black pepper

½ cup (1 stick / 113g) cold unsalted butter, cut into ¼-inch (6-mm) pieces

DIRECTIONS

1 Preheat the oven to 375°F (190°C). Generously butter a 2-quart (2-L) baking dish.

2 **Make the filling:** In a large pan, heat the olive oil and truffled olive oil, if using, over medium-high heat. Add the shallots, garlic, and bacon or pancetta, and sauté until the shallots are soft. Add the mushrooms and squash and sauté until the squash starts to soften and brown, about 15 minutes.

3 Add the parsley, sage, stock, and salt and pepper to taste; mix well. Pour the squash mixture into the prepared baking dish. Cover with foil and bake until just tender, about 30 minutes.

4 **Make the crumble topping:** Place the flour, walnuts, brown sugar, thyme, salt, and pepper to taste in a medium bowl. Add the butter and pinch with your fingers until the mixture is the consistency of coarse meal; there will still be some pea-size lumps of butter. Set the topping aside in the freezer until ready to use.

5 Remove the dish from the oven and uncover. Scatter the crumble topping over the squash and return the dish to the oven. Bake for 45 minutes more, or until the topping is golden brown. Serve warm or at room temperature.

grilled-zucchini banh mi

MAKES ABOUT 6 BANH MI

After classic grilled cheese sandwiches, our second quick go-to sandwiches are Vietnamese banh mi. Though many traditional banh mi have grilled pork and meats, we always enjoy having a vegetarian version. To make use of abundant zucchini, we'll grill up some slices of it with an Asian-style marinade and assemble a platterful for parties.

For the bread, select a light and airy baguette rather than the firmer, denser ones. One of the key elements of a great banh mi is having a bread that is crusty yet not too heavy.

INGREDIENTS

FOR THE PICKLES

1 quart (1L) warm water (just warm enough to dissolve the salt and sugar)

3 tablespoons sugar

2 tablespoons kosher or sea salt

6 tablespoons (90ml) rice vinegar

½ lb. carrots, julienned

½ lb. daikon radish, julienned

FOR THE ZUCCHINI

2 cloves garlic, crushed

3 tablespoons oil

1½ teaspoons soy sauce

½ teaspoon rice vinegar

3 medium zucchini (about 1 pound / 455g), ends trimmed

Freshly cracked black pepper

FOR THE BANH MI ASSEMBLY

2 baguettes

Fresh cilantro sprigs

Soy sauce

DIRECTIONS

1 In large pitcher or large bowl, combine the water, vinegar, sugar, and salt. Stir until the sugar and salt have dissolved and the mixture is well combined.

2 Place the carrots and daikon in a quart-size (1-L) sterilized jar (see page 55). Pour the vinegar mixture into the jar.

3 Cover the jar and refrigerate until ready to use, up to about 3 weeks. (The longer the pickles sit, the more flavorful and sour they become).

4 **Make the zucchini:** Preheat the grill. In a large bowl, combine the garlic, oil, soy sauce, and vinegar and mix well.

5 Slice the zucchini lengthwise into ¼-inch (6-mm) slices. Place the zucchini slices in the marinade and allow to marinate for 10 minutes.

6 Heat the grill and cook the zucchini slices until crisp, 2 to 3 minutes on each side.

7 Slice the baguettes in half lengthwise. On the bottom half, layer the pickles, zucchini, and cilantro, and sprinkle with soy sauce. Replace the top half of the baguettes. Cut each baguette crosswise into thirds and serve.

roasted and stuffed delicata squash rings

SERVES 2 TO 4

The first time we laid eyes on delicata squash was when we were strolling through a farmer's market in Seattle in late September. The green lines running along the length of the beautiful yellow squash were striking. We assumed it would take a while to cook, as with most other hard squashes. But the farmer reassured us that delicata skin was completely edible when roasted. So, we didn't have to peel the squash before eating it? We were sold.

When roasted, delicata squash is wonderfully tender, even with the skin on. The skin is so soft when cooked that it provides a perfect balance to the sweet flesh. It's very easy to enjoy eating the squash on its own, but we love using it as the base for a complete meal. Pairing these squash rings with different meats, vegetables, or whole grains shows the flexibility of this perfect squash.

INGREDIENTS

1 medium delicata squash, seeded and sliced in ½-inch (12-mm) rings

1 tablespoon olive oil

Kosher or sea salt and freshly cracked black pepper

FILLING OPTIONS

Basil Pesto Farro Salad (page 71)

Habanero chicken (page 194)

Almond-basil chicken (page 82)

Roasted Corn Tabouli (page 200)

DIRECTIONS

1 Preheat the oven to 450°F (230°C).

2 Rub the squash rings with the oil and season with salt and pepper to taste. Place them on a sheet pan.

3 Roast for 10 minutes, flip the rings over, and roast for 5 minutes more, or until tender.

4 Transfer the rings to a serving platter and spoon the filling of your choice into the centers.

peppers & chilies

LAYERS OF GRASSY, FRUITY, FLORAL, AND spicy notes in peppers and chilies bring food to life. Eating becomes exciting when a touch of fiery spice explodes on your palate, a smoky firecracker to awaken the senses.

When we're feeling tame, we'll harvest a handful of sweet peppers from the garden and enjoy their fruity accents in stir-fries and salads. A spectrum of sweet banana, pimento, and bell pepper colors stretch across the garden like a double rainbow after a rain. Wherever we have extra space in the garden, you'll find a mini patch of peppers ripening in the warm afternoon sun.

During periods when we're feeling daring and craving something dangerous and bold, we'll reach for a select few spicy chilies. With caution, we'll start with a few vine-ripened habaneros for wonderful spicy, fruity, floral flavors that creep slowly and warmly onto the taste buds.

Jalapeños, serranos, cayenne, goat's-weed, and Thai chilies all add quick hits of grassy-flavored heat when you're ready for a rush of adrenaline.

We've grown accustomed to using them not only to jazz up foods, but to liven up beverages as well. It takes only a chile or two to amp up a cocktail party—a few sips of spicy booze will encourage blissful conversation all evening.

A simple appetizer of charred shishito peppers and ice-cold beer embodies a brilliant balance between gentle heat and smoky sweetness. Unlike chilies used in smaller quantities, these shishito peppers are enjoyed heaped on a platter and shared among friends. The heat of shishitos is subtle and savory; they're a friendly warm-up for those wanting to delve into spicy foods, although a devilishly piquant one will surprise you every once in a while.

If you're new to eating spicy foods, we suggest you take your time and slowly develop your tolerance. These eclectic little spice bombs can deceive, and seasonally their heat levels can change from mild to extra strong. But if you're a veteran to fiery foods, be fearless and experiment with different combinations of chilies. Chile mixing can be quite exciting for lion-heated eaters.

charred bell peppers and sausage with pearled barley

SERVES 4 TO 6

Mild and nutty pearled barley adds a great chewiness and texture to one of our classic charred pepper and sausage dishes. Use any variety and color of peppers that you can get your hands on. Normally our garden has a range of sweet bell peppers growing, but recently we've been enjoying the smaller ones. The char on the peppers adds a terrific savory, smoky flavor to the whole dish, so don't be afraid to give the peppers a slight blackening.

INGREDIENTS

1 cup (200g) pearled barley

2 tablespoons olive oil

2 large bell peppers, seeded and cut into large slices

½ medium sweet onion, sliced

4 cloves garlic, crushed

1 pound (455g) uncooked sausage, pinched into small pieces

1 tablespoon fish sauce

DIRECTIONS

1 In a pot, combine the barley with 2½ cups (600ml) water. Bring to a simmer, then reduce the heat to low. Simmer, uncovered, for 35 minutes, or until the water is absorbed. Set aside.

2 Heat a large sauté pan over medium-high heat. Add the oil and pepper slices. Cook, stirring occasionally, for 5 minutes, or until the peppers have a nice char.

3 Reduce the heat to medium and add the onion, garlic, and sausage. When the sausage begins to firm up (about 1 minute), stir to lift the peppers on top of the sausage. Cook, stirring occasionally, for 5 minutes more, or until the sausage is cooked through.

4 Add the barley and fish sauce, stir to combine, and heat until the barley is warm.

sweet pepper
and teriyaki chicken skewers

SERVES 4

Sweet peppers are available year-round in different shapes and sizes. When we can get our hands on a big batch of small sweet peppers, we love adding them to our summer barbecue repertoire. It's always great to be able to grill up peppers other than the standard bell peppers. Marinated with chicken in homemade teriyaki sauce, these party-favorite sweet-pepper skewers brighten the grilling scene. They're fun to eat, and a big platter of these will empty quickly. The peppers grill up so nicely that you can just eliminate the chicken and fill the skewer with peppers for your vegetarian friends.

INGREDIENTS

Bamboo skewers

1 pound (455g) chicken cutlets, cut into 1-inch (2.5-cm) cubes

½ pound (225g) small sweet peppers or 2 bell peppers, cut into bite-size pieces

2 tablespoons vegetable oil, plus more for the grill

¼ cup (60ml) Homemade Teriyaki Sauce (page 292)

¼ cup (20g) minced fresh cilantro

DIRECTIONS

1 Soak the skewers in water for 30 minutes.

2 In a bowl, combine the chicken, peppers, oil, and teriyaki sauce.

3 Stick alternating pieces of chicken and pepper onto the skewers. Allow to marinate for 15 minutes.

4 Heat and oil the grill.

5 Place the skewers on the grill and cook, turning once, until the chicken is cooked through, about 3 minutes on each side.

6 Sprinkle with the cilantro and serve.

chile margarita
with paprika salt

MAKES 1 COCKTAIL

Rock your gathering with this drink and you will definitely not be disappointed. This is a super-fun drink for anyone who appreciates a great margarita and a nice kick of spice. It's a party in a glass—a festive blend of salt, spice, fresh lime juice, orange bitters, and, of course, our trusted tequila. Because chile peppers vary so much in heat level, take it slow and add the serrano a bit at a time. Better yet, taste the chile first to test the heat before you get your butt kicked from overspicing!

INGREDIENTS

Lime wedge
Paprika Salt (see below)
Ice
1½ ounces tequila
1½ ounces fresh lime juice
1 ounce Simple Syrup (page 74)
A few dashes orange bitters
¼ serrano chile, chopped

DIRECTIONS

1 Rub the rim of an old-fashioned cocktail glass (or other glass of your choice) with the lime wedge.

2 Put the paprika salt in a small dish and dip the rim of the glass in the paprika salt to lightly coat. Add ice cubes to the glass.

3 In a cocktail shaker filled with ice, combine the tequila, lime juice, simple syrup, bitters, and serrano. Shake vigorously for 20 seconds, then strain into the prepared glass and serve.

PAPRIKA SALT

Paprika salt is a simple 3:1 ratio of kosher or other flaky salt to paprika. It keeps well, so make as large a batch as you'd like to store. These quantities make enough to rim one glass.

1 tablespoon kosher or sea salt
1 teaspoon paprika

Mix together the salt and paprika until well combined. Store in an airtight container until ready to use.

blistered shishito peppers
with yuzu kosho

SERVES 4

During our work travels, we enjoy ending a long shoot day by visiting a local gastropub for some small flavorful plates and a few great drinks. At these little restaurant bars, blistered shishito peppers nearly always appear on the menu. It's our favorite standby appetizer order, full of flavor and fresh, spicy heat, which can vary depending on how hot the shishito peppers are. If we let our garden shishitos ripen on the vine, they turn brilliant red and superspicy. To re-create this same small-bite dish at home, we've added our version of yuzu kosho, a Japanese chile paste made from the zest of Japanese yuzu citrus. Thankfully our yuzu tree is kind to us and bears a great batch of fruit every year. If you are unable to source yuzu in your area, you can find jars of high-quality yuzu kosho at Japanese specialty markets or online.

INGREDIENTS

1 tablespoon grapeseed oil (or other neutral tasting, high-flash-point oil)

1 teaspoon Yuzu Kosho (page 255)

½ pound (225g) shishito peppers

Finely grated zest of ½ fresh lemon or yuzu

½ fresh lemon or yuzu

DIRECTIONS

1 Heat a sauté pan over high heat. Add the oil and swirl it around the pan

2 Add the yuzu kosho to the pan, stirring to spread it evenly.

3 Add the peppers to the pan and stir to coat them evenly with the yuzu kosho and oil.

4 Cook over high heat, stirring a couple times, for 3 minutes, or until the peppers are well blistered and tender.

5 Add the lemon or yuzu zest and stir to combine evenly.

6 Remove from the heat and plate. Squeeze fresh lemon or yuzu juice over the peppers, to taste. Serve immediately.

HABANERO CHICKEN TACOS PAGE 194
SPICY RADISH SALSA PAGE 116

habanero chicken tacos

SERVES 4

In our younger years, we really loved our spicy foods and could tolerate serious levels of heat. Now that we're older, our bodies can handle only subtler levels, but we still crave the wonderful fire of habaneros. These chile peppers have terrific floral and fruity notes, enhancing any flavors they touch. Life without spicy food would be extremely bland and boring for us, so the extra kick of habanero keeps us young. For these chicken tacos, add small amounts of habanero at a time; each chile can vary in spice level. But if you're a spice addict with a strong stomach, go for a few whole chilies—at your own risk. Be as brave as you want with the chile, but don't forget to preserve your taste buds for your next meal.

INGREDIENTS

2 tablespoons vegetable oil

1 small onion, chopped

2 cloves garlic, minced

1 pound (455g) chicken cutlets, cut into 1-inch (2.5-cm) cubes

1 red bell pepper, seeded and sliced into 2-inch (5-cm) strips

¼ teaspoon kosher or sea salt

Freshly cracked black pepper

1 teaspoon Worcestershire sauce

1 habanero chile, seeded and thinly sliced

Tortillas

Fresh cilantro, chopped

Optional fillings: chopped red onion, shredded cheese, sour cream, sliced avocado, or Spicy Radish Salsa (page 116)

DIRECTIONS

1 In a large pan, heat the oil over medium heat. Add the onion and garlic and cook until soft. Add the chicken, bell pepper, salt, pepper to taste, and Worcestershire sauce. Raise the heat to medium-high and cook for 10 minutes.

2 Slowly add slices of habanero to reach your desired level of spiciness. Continue cooking for another 2 minutes, or until the chicken is cooked through.

3 Warm the tortillas, wrapped in foil, in the oven or char them by holding them one or two at a time with a pair of tongs over the flame of a gas cooktop, flipping them over every few seconds until both sides are charred. Fill the tortillas with the chicken and top with the cilantro. If desired, add other fillings of your choice. Fold the tacos over and serve.

homemade sriracha (chile hot sauce)

MAKES ABOUT 1 CUP (240ML)

If you love the bottled versions of different Sriracha hot sauces, then making your own at home will be life changing. Not only will you able to customize your Sriracha's blend of spiciness, sweetness, and tang, but you'll also find that the fresh flavors coming from vine-ripened chilies are fantastic. We first shared a homemade Sriracha recipe on our blog years ago, and it was so well received that readers shared their own special variations. So go "outside the bottle" and try your own homemade batch.

This recipe's spiciness will vary depending on the chilies. Start your first batch with smaller quantities of chile peppers to familiarize yourself with their heat level and to learn your own preference.

INGREDIENTS

1 tablespoon vegetable oil

4 to 5 medium cloves garlic, crushed or minced

2 medium shallots, minced

2 (8-ounce / 227-g) cans tomato sauce

1 cup (about 100g) Thai red chile peppers, or to taste (start with half this amount for a milder sauce), stemmed and minced fine (see Notes)

1 tablespoon fish sauce (see Notes)

3 tablespoons rice vinegar

3 tablespoons sugar

NOTES Wear rubber gloves to protect your skin when mincing the peppers. The smaller the mince, the smoother your final sauce will be.

Don't skimp on the fish sauce! If you really can't find it, you may substitute soy sauce.

DIRECTIONS

1 In a saucepan, heat the oil over medium-high heat, then add the garlic and shallots. Sauté for 1 minute, or just until the shallots are light brown and fragrant (don't burn your garlic!).

2 Add the tomato sauce and chilies. Let the sauce come to a simmer, then lower the heat to keep the mixture at a low simmer. Add the fish sauce, vinegar, and sugar. Mix well.

3 Continue simmering the sauce for about 5 minutes. This will break down the chilies and soften them, to create a smooth consistency.

4 Remove from the heat and allow to cool completely.

5 Transfer the sauce to a blender and blend on "liquefy" or a similar setting until the sauce is smooth, or until most of the pepper skins and seeds have broken down and been incorporated.

6 Taste the hot sauce and add more fish sauce, sugar, vinegar, or water to taste. Blend one last time, until very smooth. Pour the sauce into a sterilized jar (see page 55) and refrigerate for up to 1 month.

other vegetable fruits

PLUMP, TENDER EGGPLANT. FRESH, CRISP cucumbers. Juicy, sweet corn. How drab summertime would be without all of this wonderful produce. Picnics would suffer and backyard gatherings would falter without some inspiration from these vegetable fruits.

They all join the list of foods—such as tomatoes, peas, chilies, and squash—that have had a confusing time being defined as either a vegetable or a fruit. Botanists raise their fists in unison declaring them fruits, yet due to their popular use in savory dishes, those in the culinary world have insisted they are vegetables. The argument was even brought before the Supreme Court in 1893 to determine the correct answer! In the end, classification should matter little; what is of consequence is the delight these wonderful plants provide.

Corn is the one member of this family that is nearly universally embraced. Put it on the table and you'll almost never hear, "Oh, I don't like corn." Even with its prevalence in our baskets and gardens, the taste of fresh summer corn never grows tiring. Whenever you bite into an ear of corn, you're treated to sweet little explosions of flavor from every kernel. Even the smell is intoxicating when you're husking fresh corn cobs.

The elongated ovals of eggplants have always had a spot in our garden. Beginning with the classic Black Beauties, we gradually started to explore other varieties. Long, slender Japanese eggplants and the beautifully gradiated Rosa Biancas have thrived in our garden beds, delighting us with their delicate flavors.

With many of the smaller, more tender eggplants, there is no need to salt them before cooking, and the seeds are small and unobtrusive. Their texture is creamy, and when grilled or seared they provide a beautiful contrast on the palate between their thin, crisped skins and their delicate flesh. They readily pick up hints of smoke from the barbecue and marry beautifully with accompanying ingredients.

Cucumbers tend to elicit love-hate relationships, and the occasional tough, seedy, mushy-centered cucumber does little to help win the love. A fresh, crisp cucumber is glorious, however; it can inspire cravings and become the hero of a salad. The smaller varieties, often labeled as Persian or Japanese cucumbers, are incredible. They have such a clean flavor and amazing crunch, in addition to being seedless (or *parthenocarpic*, meaning "having virgin fruit"). Although we struggle with growing them, they are a staple in our household; the struggle just makes us appreciate them all the more when we buy them from favorite farmers and markets.

Whether on grill tops or in dips and salads, these vegetable fruits leave us happy, satisfied, and basking in the glory of summer. They will always find a home in our picnics and on our feast tables.

roasted-corn tabouli

SERVES 6

Homemade tabouli made with a mix of fresh parley and mint leaves is such a treat, especially when we add in roasted corn. The sweet pops of corn kernels in this salad make it one of the highlights of summer. If you really love your corn, just double the amount of roasted corn in the recipe. You won't be disappointed.

INGREDIENTS

1 cup (140g) uncooked bulgur

3 medium ears corn, husks and kernels removed

¼ cup (60ml) vegetable oil

½ cup (30g) chopped fresh flat-leaf parsley

½ cup (40g) chopped fresh mint leaves

Zest of 1 lemon

3 tablespoons fresh lemon juice

1 teaspoon kosher or sea salt

¼ teaspoon cayenne

Freshly cracked black pepper

DIRECTIONS

1 Preheat the oven 450°F (230°C).

2 In a saucepan, combine the bulgur with 2 cups (480ml) water. Bring the water to a boil, then remove the pan from the heat. Cover, and allow to sit for 20 minutes, until the water has been absorbed. Set aside to cool.

3 In a bowl, combine the corn kernels with 2 tablespoons of the oil and toss to coat. Arrange the kernels in a single layer on a baking sheet and roast for 8 to 10 minutes, or until cooked through. Allow to cool.

4 In a large bowl, combine the bulgur, corn kernels, parsley, and mint. In small bowl, combine the lemon zest, lemon juice, remaining 2 tablespoons oil, salt, cayenne, and pepper to taste.

5 Add the lemon juice mixture into the corn mixture and chill for 15 minutes before serving.

cucumber mint quinoa salad
with shallot vinaigrette

SERVES 4 TO 6

We're still trying to figure out why we've never had a successful cucumber-growing season. Normally we'll get a batch of about ten cucumbers that look great, but after that, our cucumber vines fizzle into oblivion. We're still not giving up, and hopefully one year we'll have enough to satisfy our cucumber cravings. It's salads like this one that really let cucumbers shine and make us crave them even more; it's full of crunchy freshness, and the mint-quinoa combination makes it a perfect summer picnic dish to share with friends.

INGREDIENTS

FOR THE SHALLOT DRESSING
¼ cup (60ml) olive or grapeseed oil

3 large shallots, minced

3 medium cloves garlic, minced

2 teaspoons sugar

2 tablespoons soy sauce

1 teaspoon sesame oil

¼ teaspoon kosher or sea salt

1 tablespoon rice vinegar

1 tablespoon fresh lemon juice

Freshly cracked black pepper

FOR THE SALAD
1 cup (170g) raw quinoa (see Note)

1 cup (135g) diced cucumber

½ cup (40g) chopped fresh mint leaves, or more to taste

DIRECTIONS

1 Make the shallot dressing: In a saucepan, heat 2 tablespoons of the olive or grapeseed oil over medium-low heat. Add the shallots and garlic and cook until a light golden brown or until fragrant, about 2 minutes. Immediately remove the pan from the heat and add the remaining 2 tablespoons olive or grapeseed oil, the sugar, soy sauce, sesame oil, salt, vinegar, lemon juice, and pepper to taste. Stir until the sugar dissolves and all the ingredients are well combined. Set aside to marinate briefly.

2 Make the salad: In a saucepan, combine the quinoa with 2 cups (480ml) water. Bring to a simmer, cover, then reduce the heat to low and cook for 15 minutes, or until the water is fully absorbed. Place the cooled quinoa in a large bowl. Add the cucumbers and chopped mint and stir to combine.

3 Add the shallot dressing and toss well to coat. Serve immediately, or chill in the refrigerator and toss again before serving.

NOTE For a warm quinoa dish, toss the cucumbers and herbs with the quinoa while it is still warm. Prepare the dressing as instructed and toss with the warm quinoa mixture. Serve immediately.

miso-sesame cucumber salad

SERVES 2 TO 3

When eating at our local Japanese *izakaya* restaurants, we always look forward to the cucumber salad amuses-bouches that they greet us with at the table. It's such a treat to be able to snack on fresh cucumbers laced with delicate Japanese flavors. Inspired by those simple cucumber salads, we've re-created our own version with Japanese miso paste. The salty and deep umami flavors balance so well with the fresh crispness of cucumbers. If possible, try to find crunchy Persian or Japanese cucumbers. They don't have tough seeds and can be eaten whole.

INGREDIENTS

½ pound (225g) crisp cucumbers, preferably Japanese or Persian variety

½ cup (80g) red onion, thinly sliced

2 tablespoons vegetable or grapeseed oil

1 teaspoon sesame oil

1 tablespoon fresh lime juice

1 teaspoon miso paste

1 teaspoon soy sauce

1 teaspoon sugar

1 tablespoon rice vinegar

Toasted sesame seeds, for garnish (optional)

DIRECTIONS

1 In a large bowl, combine the cucumbers and red onion. Set aside.

2 In a medium bowl, combine the vegetable or grapeseed oil, sesame oil, lime juice, miso paste, soy sauce, sugar, and vinegar. Combine well.

3 Add the miso mixture to the bowl with the cucumbers. Toss together to evenly coat. Chill for about 20 minutes.

4 Just before serving, sprinkle with the sesame seeds, if desired.

grilled japanese eggplants with orange zest and sake glaze

SERVES 4

Japanese eggplants are easily one of our favorite varieties for grilling. Their slender size, delicate seeds, and thin skins are perfect for quick summertime barbecuing. They also tend to be less bitter than their larger cousins, like Black Beauty eggplants, so there is no need to salt them before cooking (see Note). The sugars in the glaze will burn quickly, so for this recipe, cook both sides of the eggplants most of the way through, glaze the eggplants, then cook the glazed sides for just a minute to caramelize the glaze.

INGREDIENTS

4 medium Japanese eggplants (about 1 pound / 455g), halved lengthwise

Vegetable oil

¼ cup (60ml) sake

1 tablespoon miso, preferably white (*shiro*) miso

2 tablespoons sugar

1 tablespoon honey (preferably orange blossom)

Finely grated zest of 1 large orange (about 1 tablespoon)

1 tablespoon orange juice

NOTE If you're using thicker eggplants, cut them into thick steaks to grill; you may need to salt them to extract some of their bitter liquid.

DIRECTIONS

1 Heat the grill for high-heat direct grilling.

2 Score the eggplants several times on their cut sides and brush with oil. Set aside.

3 In a small saucepan, combine the sake, miso, sugar, and honey. Bring to a simmer over medium-high heat to dissolve the miso and sugar and to cook off a bit of the alcohol from the sake. When the glaze reaches a simmer, remove from the heat. Stir in the orange zest and orange juice.

4 Brush the grill grates with oil to help prevent sticking.

5 Place the eggplants, cut side down, on the grill. Cook for 2 to 3 minutes, then flip the eggplants over. Brush the cut sides with about one-third of the glaze.

6 Cook, cut side up, for 2 to 3 minutes. Flip again and brush the skin sides of the eggplants with another one-third of the glaze.

7 Cook for 1 minute. Flip again and lightly brush the cut sides one more time with the remaining glaze. Cook, cut side up, for 1 minute to finish caramelizing the glaze on the skin sides of the eggplants.

8 Remove from the heat and serve.

chunky roasted eggplant and parmesan dip

SERVES 4

When tender, purple globe eggplants come into season, this is a healthy dip that satisfies our cravings to snack with a minimum of calorie guilt. Made from roasted eggplants and fresh yogurt, it pairs well with celery and carrot sticks or your favorite whole-grain cracker. Yes, there's Parmesan in the dip, but it brings out the zesty flavor. So consider it a compromise—it's a *mostly* healthy dip. Enjoy!

INGREDIENTS

Olive oil

1 medium purple globe eggplant (about 1 pound / 455g)

Sea salt

Freshly cracked black pepper

½ cup (120ml) yogurt

½ teaspoon fresh lemon juice

½ cup (50g) freshly grated Parmesan

1 teaspoon red pepper flakes

Crackers or chips, for serving

DIRECTIONS

1 Preheat the oven to 350°F (175°C). Brush a sheet pan with oil.

2 Slice the eggplant into rounds ½ inch (12 mm) thick. Coat both sides of the slices with salt and set aside for about 30 minutes, to draw out the bitterness of the eggplant.

3 Rinse the slices to remove the salt. Blot dry with paper towels.

4 On the prepared sheet pan, arrange the eggplant in a single layer. Brush with oil. Season to taste with pepper.

5 Roast for 30 minutes, or until the eggplant is soft. About halfway through roasting, flip the slices over on the sheet pan.

6 Allow the eggplant to cool. Remove the peels and the seeds.

7 In a blender, combine the eggplant pulp, ¼ teaspoon salt, the yogurt, lemon juice, Parmesan, and red pepper flakes. Blend to the consistency you prefer. (We prefer our dip on the slightly chunky side.)

8 Chill the dip for about 30 minutes. Serve with crackers or chips of your choosing.

corn fritters

MAKES 18 (3-INCH / 7.5-CM) FRITTERS

This appetizer brings back some great memories. One of the very first meals we cooked together was these crispy corn fritters. We spent the early part of the evening making a fun little mess in the kitchen. But what we ended up with was such a huge batch of sweet corn fritters that we saved them for sandwiches for the next few days. To this day, it's still one of our favorite ways to savor sweet summer corn as a finger food or party snack. We like to dip these in our homemade barbecue sauce (page 56) or a blue cheese buttermilk dip.

INGREDIENTS

3 cups (495g) fresh corn kernels (from about 3 ears)

1 medium sweet onion (about ½ pound / 225g), diced

4 cloves garlic, crushed

½ cup (15g) roughly chopped fresh flat-leaf parsley

3 tablespoons unsalted butter, melted

1½ teaspoons baking powder

½ teaspoon kosher or sea salt

½ teaspoon freshly cracked black pepper

4 eggs

¼ cup (60ml) milk

1¼ cups (155g) flour

Vegetable oil, for frying

DIRECTIONS

1 In a large bowl, mix together the corn, onion, garlic, parsley, butter, baking powder, salt, and pepper.

2 Add the eggs and milk. Stir until well combined. Mix in the flour.

3 In a large sauté pan, heat ½ inch (12 mm) of oil over medium-high heat. Drop spoonfuls of batter into the oil to form fritters, flattening the tops slightly. Do not crowd the pan.

4 Cook for 2 minutes on each side, or until golden. Drain the fritters on paper towels.

5 Repeat with the rest of the batter, adding more oil if necessary. When adding oil between batches, make sure it comes up to temperature before cooking more fritters. Also, be sure to scoop out stray corn kernels between batches of fritters. The strays will overheat and pop, splattering hot oil.

6 Serve warm, with your preferred dipping sauce.

italian-style fried okra

SERVES 4 TO 6

From Todd Most people seem to have a love-hate relationship with okra. When cooked, it can develop a bit of an unappealing slimy texture. Like Grandma used to say, however, "It isn't that you don't like something, it is just that you haven't found a way it's prepared in which you do." What better way to convert someone into an okra lover than by serving it to them nicely battered and fried? This Italian-style batter is our absolute favorite for frying veggies: light and crisp, with white wine and nutmeg giving it a special sweetness. Make sure the oil is nice and hot before frying, or the okra will come out oily. The resting period after dipping the okra in the batter allows the excess batter to drip off and also helps bind the batter to the surface of the okra. Without that time, the okra will often slip out of the crust when you bite into it. The batter works equally well for just about any vegetable or meat you like to fry.

INGREDIENTS

DIRECTIONS

FOR THE BATTER
2 cups (250g) flour
½ teaspoon kosher or sea salt
Freshly grated nutmeg
Freshly cracked black pepper
¼ cup (60ml) olive oil
2 eggs, separated
½ cup (120ml) dry white wine

FOR THE OKRA
2 pounds (910g) whole okra
Vegetable oil, for frying
Sea salt
Fresh lemon wedges, for serving

1 **Make the batter:** In a medium bowl, whisk together the flour, salt, and nutmeg and pepper to taste. Make a well in the center, then whisk in the olive oil and egg yolks until some of the flour is incorporated.

2 Add the wine to the well and whisk until some more of the flour is incoporated. Add 1 cup (240ml) water and whisk until the batter is smooth. If you have time, resting the batter in the fridge for 2 hours will yield the best texture, but you can use it right away if you need to.

3 In a separate bowl (preferably a copper one), whisk the eggs whites until stiff. Gently fold the egg whites into the batter.

4 **Make the okra:** Dip the okra into the batter to coat completely and place on a wire rack for 15 minutes.

5 In a large frying pan, heat 1 inch (2.5 cm) of oil to 375°F (190°C). Fry the okra in batches for 3 to 5 minutes, or until golden. Drain on paper towels, sprinkle with sea salt, and serve with lemon wedges.

tomatillo salsa

Ever since we witnessed a tomatillo salsa being made at home, we were hooked for life. Our photographer friend Penny De Los Santos took us to meet a friend of hers in East Los Angeles who is known as "The Barbacoa Lady." This lovely woman specializes in making lamb barbacoa, and though we didn't have any that morning, she made us an incredible lunch of chicharrones tacos and tomatillo salsa. The fresh tomatillos were roasted to a fragrant char in a dry pan, then crushed in her *molcajete*. Everything was made by hand and tasted incredible. So, this recipe is inspired by The Barbacoa Lady, who showed us how a simple technique, some ingenuity, and lots of love can make a simple side dish amazing.

INGREDIENTS

1 pound (455g) medium tomatillos, husks removed

1 small onion, cut into quarters

3 cloves garlic

1 jalapeño or serrano chile

1 Anaheim or poblano chile

½ teaspoon kosher or sea salt

1 teaspoon fresh lime juice

½ cup (30g) minced fresh cilantro

Chips, for serving

DIRECTIONS

1 Wash the tomatillos well to remove any stickiness. Dry well.

2 Pan roast the tomatillos: In a large, dry pan, add the tomatillos and turn the heat to medium. The skins of the tomatillos will start to brown, then char. Cook, turning the tomatillos frequently, until the tops and bottoms are brown. Remove the tomatillos from the pan and allow to cool.

3 In the same heated pan, add the onion, garlic, and chilies and dry roast them in the pan. Gently stir the ingredients until they are brown and roasted. Remove from the heat and allow to cool.

4 Remove the stems from the chilies and add them to a blender with the tomatillos, onion-garlic mixture, salt, lime juice, and cilantro. Blend until well combined.

5 Add additional salt or chile to taste. Or add a little water, if needed, to thin out the salsa.

6 Serve with chips.

fruit

SWEET BERRIES · CITRUS · STONE FRUITS
OTHER TREE & VINE FRUITS

sweet berries

IS THERE ANYTHING MORE PLEASING THAN A freshly picked berry? A delicate raspberry gently plucked from the vine or a basket of strawberries from your favorite farmer's stand? The scents of the berries fill the car as you drive home, enticing you to reach over and grab a handful.

When it comes to the berries in our garden, it feels like we spend half our time competing with the animals to get our fair share. The army of squirrels, birds, and dogs easily have us outnumbered. We initially grew our strawberries as ground cover, with the fruit as an added treat. We had imagined ourselves stepping out into the garden first thing in the morning and picking a handful of strawberries to enjoy with our breakfast.

That notion remained a fantasy because our first Rhodesian Ridgeback, Dante, quickly discovered how much he liked them and started rising bright and early to have a pre-breakfast snack. We do, however, have his voracious berry appetite to thank for helping us develop a sharing attitude. The same birds that steal our blueberries also help control the bugs in the garden. The squirrels are kind of cute munching on the berries, and they give our pups a workout trying to protect said berries. We can't walk by the strawberry patch without sweet memories of Dante foraging for his daily breakfast.

Over the years we've been fortunate enough to find more types of berries that grow in our climate than we had originally thought. Raspberries and blueberries have now found a home in our garden—two fruits we had initially given up on.

Despite all the berries we are able to grow, we'll travel insane distances to track down particularly exquisite varieties. Take a summer road trip through Oregon or Washington and you'll find brambles of blackberries growing like weeds all over the hillsides. And once you experience a marionberry, your taste buds will be changed for life. This has fueled our inspiration to grow them in the garden and use them in the kitchen. Cocktails, pastries, and desserts filled with sweet berries all reign among our favorites. We just need to plant plenty of extras to make sure we have enough for the animals *and* ourselves.

blackberry cabernet crisp
with honeyed whipped cream

SERVES 6 TO 8

Granted, we don't live in the best berry-growing country, but when we found some blackberry vines suitable for our region, we were like giddy kids in a candy store. We're just silly that way, prancing around like puppies about to get a treat when we find we can grow a small handful of berries.

We're starting to enjoy our newly planted blackberry vines, and as they produce more fruit over the years, we look forward to many more homegrown versions of this fantastic crisp. The rich flavors of cabernet complement the blackberries perfectly, adding an extra layer of depth to the fruit. Of course anytime you're baking with wine, make sure to pour an extra glass for yourself.

INGREDIENTS

Butter, for the baking dish

FOR THE FILLING
6 cups (1½ to 2 pounds / 680 to 910g) blackberries

1 cup (240ml) red wine, preferably cabernet

1 cup (200g) sugar

½ cup (60g) flour

FOR THE TOPPING
½ cup (60g) flour

¼ cup (55g) packed brown sugar

½ teaspoon kosher or sea salt

¼ cup (½ stick / 57g) cold unsalted butter, cut into ½-inch (12-mm) pieces

½ cup (40g) old-fashioned oats

FOR THE WHIPPED CREAM
1 cup (60ml) heavy cream

1 tablespoon honey

1 teaspoon vanilla extract

2 tablespoons confectioners' sugar

DIRECTIONS

1 Preheat the oven to 375°F (190°C). Butter a 2-quart (2-L) baking dish or several small dishes of equivalent volume.

2 **Make the filling:** In a bowl, combine all the filling ingredients. Spread the mixture in the baking dish(es). Set aside.

3 **Make the topping:** In a bowl, combine the flour, brown sugar, and salt. Using your fingertips, pinch the butter pieces into the flour until the texture is crumbly. Pinch in the oats and work with your fingertips until the ingredients are evenly mixed and the topping is in small clumps (see Note).

4 Spread the topping over the blackberry filling. Bake for 45 minutes, or until golden.

5 **Make the whipped cream:** In a bowl, whip together the cream, honey, vanilla extract, and confectioners' sugar until the mixture forms soft peaks (when you lift the whisk out of the cream, a peak should form and then gently fall back, barely holding its shape).

NOTE If you have finished this step before your oven is pre-heated, place the topping in the freezer for a few minutes to chill. When the oven reaches temperature, remove the topping from the freezer and proceed with the instructions. The chilling will give the topping an extra crispness when baked.

Place the whipped cream in a covered container and reserve in the fridge until ready to serve.

6 Remove the crisp from oven and set aside to cool for at least 15 minutes. Serve warm or at room temperature topped with the whipped cream.

roasted-strawberry scones

MAKES 10 SCONES

In the peak of spring, our little strawberry patch is bursting with berries and it always brings back memories of our first dog, Dante. He would rush out every morning to eat the first ripened berries of the day, and the only way we could beat him to any strawberries was to wake up really early ourselves. We're not quite that ambitious, so instead, we enjoyed our sleep and loved knowing that he was able to enjoy his morning treats.

INGREDIENTS

½ pound (225g) strawberries, hulled and cut into halves and quarters

1 tablespoon brown sugar

¼ teaspoon freshly cracked black pepper

2½ cups (310g) flour

½ cup (100g) sugar

1 tablespoon baking powder

Finely grated zest of 1 medium lemon

½ teaspoon kosher or sea salt

6 tablespoons (¾ stick / 90g) cold unsalted butter, cut into ½-inch (12-mm) pieces

1 egg

1 egg yolk

¾ cup (180ml) heavy cream

Preserves, for serving

DIRECTIONS

1 Preheat the oven to 375°F (190°C). Line three sheet pans with parchment paper.

2 In a bowl, combine the strawberries, brown sugar, and pepper and toss to coat. Spread the mixture out over one of the lined sheet pans.

3 Roast for 30 minutes. Remove from the oven and set aside to cool. Keep the oven on.

4 In a large bowl, whisk together the flour, sugar, baking powder, lemon zest, and salt for at least 20 seconds. Using your fingertips, pinch the butter into the flour mixture until most of the big chunks are broken down.

5 In a separate bowl, whisk together the egg, egg yolk, and cream. Make a well in the middle of the flour, and pour the cream mixture into the well. Incorporate the cream into the flour by stirring from the inside of the well and slowly working outward until the flour is just combined (do not overmix).

6 Gently form the batter into disks 2½ inches (6 cm) in diameter and 1 inch (2.5 cm) high. With your fingertips, make four or five indentations on the top of each scone and place a roasted strawberry in each. Place the scones about 1 inch (2.5 cm) apart on the two remaining lined sheet pans. Bake for 20 to 25 minutes, or until light golden.

7 Serve with preserves.

mixed berry chocolate slab pie

MAKES 1 (13-BY-18-INCH / 32.5-BY-45-CM) PIE

This is a massive slab pie, which will easily serve a small army—or a few ravenous teenagers. Consider it a community pie, where everyone can contribute berries for the baking or come help you eat. Either way, it's the easiest way to feed a lot of folks a great slice of pie from one hearty baking dish. Everyone will be swooning over the size, the flavor, and all the chocolate in each slice.

   At first it may seem intimidating to roll the dough so large and transfer it to the pans, but this dough handles quite easily, and if you happen to break it, you can patch it with dough scraps. If you have fewer people to feed, you can always halve the recipe and use a smaller pan, but there are always neighbors who will take leftovers, so we encourage you to give the full recipe a shot!

INGREDIENTS

FOR THE FILLING

3 pounds (1.4kg) mixed fresh
   berries, larger berries halved
   or quartered

1 cup (200g) sugar

3 tablespoons cornstarch

1½ cups (250g) chocolate chips

FOR THE CRUST

8 cups (1kg) flour

1 cup (200g) sugar

2 teaspoons kosher or sea salt

1 pound (455g) cold unsalted
   butter, cut into ½-inch (12-mm)
   pieces

3 eggs

½ cup (120ml) cold water

Heavy cream, for brushing
   the crust

Confectioners' sugar, for dusting
   (optional)

DIRECTIONS

1 Preheat the oven to 400°F (205°C). Butter one 13-by-18-inch (33- by-46-cm) sheet pan. Set aside another to use as a template.

2 **Start the filling:** Put the berries in a large bowl. In a small bowl, whisk together the sugar and cornstarch until well combined. Add the sugar mixture to the berries and gently toss. Set aside.

3 **Make the crust:** In a large bowl, whisk together the flour, sugar, and salt. Pinching with your fingers or using a pastry blender, incorporate the butter into the mixture until no large pieces of butter remain and the mixture has a crumbly texture.

4 In a separate bowl, whisk the eggs with the cold water. Make a well in the middle of the flour mixture, then pour the egg mixture into the well. Working from the center out, combine the egg and flour mixtures until the dough holds together. If necessary, adjust by adding a little additional flour or cold water if the dough is too sticky or not holding together.

5 Divide the dough into two portions, one twice the size of the other.

recipe continues

6 On a large floured surface, roll out the larger portion of dough to an 18-by-22-inch (45-by-55-cm) rectangle (we usually roll it out slightly larger, then trim the edges straight to the correct dimensions). Dust the underside and the top of the dough with flour a few times while rolling out to keep the dough from sticking.

7 Gently wrap the dough around the rolling pin, then unroll it over the first sheet pan. Adjust the dough so it sits evenly in the sheet pan. Dock the pastry by pressing down with your fingertips several times, making indentations across the bottom of the pastry. Spread the chocolate chips in an even layer over the pastry. Spread the berry mixture in an even layer on top of the chips. Set aside.

8 Roll out the smaller dough portion to a rectangle just larger than 13 by 18 inches (32.5 by 45 cm). Flip the second sheet pan upside down and gently press it into the dough, then lift the pan off. Use the impression to cut the dough to size. Gently wrap it around the rolling pin, then unroll it over the slab pie to form a top crust.

9 Fold excess dough from the crust bottom up and around to meet the pie top and gently pinch the crust to form the top edge. Brush the top and the edges of the pastry with cream. Using kitchen scissors or a knife, cut slits into the top of the slab pie.

10 Bake for 30 to 40 minutes, or until the top is golden. Remove the pie from the oven and allow to cool. Dust with confectioners' sugar (if desired), slice, and serve.

blueberry frangipane tarts

MAKES 6 INDIVIDUAL TARTS

Behold, a dessert to satisfy all those blueberry lovers in your life! Simple, rustic, stylish, and studded with blueberries, these frangipane tarts are perfect for breakfast. But using blueberries in these versatile tarts is just one of the many variations that we churn out of the oven. Try using strawberries, raspberries, or even apples and pears, for an autumn touch. It can be difficult to decide what fruit to use, but rest assured that whichever you choose, these tarts will be a favorite on your baking list.

INGREDIENTS

FOR THE CRUST

2 cups (250g) flour

¾ cup (1½ sticks / 170g) cold unsalted butter, cut into ½-inch (12-mm) pieces

½ teaspoon kosher or sea salt

1 tablespoon sugar

1 egg

¼ cup (60ml) cold water

FOR THE FILLING

½ cup (1 stick / 113g) unsalted butter at room temperature

½ cup (100g) sugar

2 cups (200g) ground almonds

Pinch of kosher or sea salt

2 tablespoons orange liqueur (such as Grand Marnier)

2 eggs

1½ cups (250g) blueberries

Confectioners' sugar, for dusting

DIRECTIONS

1 Preheat the oven to 375°F (190°C). Set aside six 4- or 4¾-inch (10- or 12-cm) tartlet pans.

2 **Make the crust:** In a medium bowl, using your fingertips, pinch together the flour, butter, salt, and sugar until most of the big chunks of butter are flattened or broken up.

3 In a bowl, whisk the egg with the cold water until combined. Mix the egg into the flour mixture until the flour binds together and forms a rough ball (gently knead the ball to incorporate the last of the flour).

4 Divide the ball into six equal pieces (about 3 ounces / 90g each). Roll each piece into a ball, then flatten each slightly into a disk. Place the disks in the freezer for 5 minutes.

5 On a lightly floured surface, roll the disks out to 6 inches (15 cm) in diameter. Fit them into the tartlet pans, pressing the dough into the sides. Press off the excess dough around the tops of the pans. Dock the bottoms of the tartlets, making small indentations with the tips of your fingers. Set aside in the fridge until the filling is made.

recipe continues

6 **Make the filling:** In a stand mixer fitted with the paddle attachment, beat the butter on medium speed until creamy. Beat in the sugar. Reduce the mixer speed to low and beat in the ground almonds, salt, and orange liqueur. Add the eggs one at a time, and beat until fully incorporated.

7 Divide the almond mixture evenly among the tartlet crusts, filling them three-quarters full. Divide the blueberries among the tarts, slightly pressing some of the berries deeper into the batter.

8 Bake for 30 minutes, or until the crust is golden around the edges. Allow to cool. Remove the tarts from the pans, dust with confectioners' sugar, and serve.

casanova cocktail

MAKES 2 COCKTAILS

Friends, this drink is a sexy beast. So get ready to impress some ladies, or gentlemen. Muddled raspberries and a touch of orange bitters make the perfect celebratory and romantic Champagne drink. It's a simple yet stylish cocktail that you can share with good friends when you ring in the new year, or delight a loved one with on an intimate evening date. The few dashes of orange bitters add an extra layer of depth to this elegant cocktail.

INGREDIENTS	DIRECTIONS
10 fresh raspberries	1 In a small bowl or bartender's glass, muddle the raspberries, simple syrup, and orange bitters together.
1 ounce Simple Syrup (page 74)	
Few dashes orange bitters	2 Pour the fruit mixture into two Champagne flutes, then top with Champagne.
8 ounces Champagne or Cava Brut	

marionberry mojito ice pops

MAKES 13 (4-INCH) ICE POPS

Offer us a bowl of sweet, vine-ripened blackberries and we'll attack it with ferocity. It's embarrassing, we know, this crazy berry-obsessed behavior. But until you've had a fresh, plump, sun-ripened blackberry, gently plucked off its vine, you shouldn't laugh at us too loudly.

Among the masses of blackberry varieties, marionberries reign. Described as the cabernet of blackberries, they have a deep, rich flavor. They have all the classic blackberry traits—a touch of tartness balancing their berry sweetness—but the same deep complexity of flavor Cabernet wines often have. If you can find marionberries, these ice pops will be extraordinary, but even with regular blackberries they are incredibly good.

These are adult pops. We've yet to adjust the recipe to make a zero-proof ice pop, but if you want to go that route, start by replacing the rum with water, then increase the lime juice or simple syrup if necessary.

INGREDIENTS

13 ice pop sticks

1½ cups (200g) fresh or frozen marionberries (if unavailable, use regular blackberries)

½ cup (120ml) fresh lime juice

½ cup (120ml) rum

¾ cup (180ml) Simple Syrup (page 74), or more to taste

Several hearty dashes of bitters of your choice (we usually use orange)

20 to 25 large mint leaves

Ice pop molds

NOTE Depending on the blender, the fruit mixture may develop a frothy layer after being blended. If so, allow the bubbles to settle and pop before pouring the fruit mixture into the molds.

DIRECTIONS

1 If using wooden ice pop sticks, soak the sticks in warm water for 1 hour before making the pops (this keeps them from floating when inserted in the molds).

2 Place the berries in a blender or a food processor. (If using frozen berries, thaw before blending.)

3 Add all the remaining ingredients and ½ cup (120ml) water to the berries. Pulse until the mint is finely chopped.

4 Taste for sweetness and add more simple syrup if necessary (it should be a touch too sweet because it will lose sweetness once frozen).

5 Pour the fruit mixture into the molds (see Note) and insert a stick in the center of each. (If you prefer a seed-free, no-pulp consistency, strain the mixture through a fine-mesh sieve before pouring it into the molds.)

6 Freeze for 4 hours, or until completely solid. Unmold before serving (run warm water around the molds if necessary to help the pops release).

citrus

BELOVED CITRUS. GIVEN OUR TEMPERATE Southern California climate, citrus quickly became the foundation of our garden. We built planters to raise the semi-dwarfs onto a pedestal and allow their roots to stretch and meander. We designed curved pathways to bring visitors brushing past the sweet scents of lemon blossoms. We placed trellises where the candylike tangerines could overgrow and dangle their fruit within easy grasp.

Because we have had the good fortune to be able to grow our own citrus, it's nearly impossible not to be infatuated with them. There truly is nothing like citrus picked fresh off the tree: oranges packed with sweet juices that drip down your forearms as you cut them open, lemons with oils so saturated in their rinds that with one slice they can be smelled across the room, a tangerine left on the tree to sweeten through midsummer, gently warmed by the sun and enjoyed alongside a morning cappuccino.

Citrus plays a vital role in our daily eating and drinking. Life without citrus is like life without music or sunshine. It brings joy and brightness into the kitchen and onto our plates. Just think of all of the diverse recipes you're able to create using citrus: warm lemon madeleine cookies nestled onto a plate and served with hot tea. Brilliant orange kumquat marmalade spread atop English muffins or served next to slices of brie. Cocktails, dressings, and desserts seem almost unthinkable without the use of citrus zest, juice, and flesh.

Those able to find or grow some of the less common varieties can take an already delicious dish to extraordinary heights. A watercress salad with the addition of some slices of oro blanco (a grapefruit-pomelo cross) is unforgettable. The less acidic floral offspring of the grapefruit lends a perfect balance of sweetness and tartness to the dish.

Tasting a fresh yuzu is an extraordinary experience. I remember slicing open the first one off our tree. Diane was coming down the hall, more than thirty feet away, and exclaimed, "What is that amazing smell?" That fragrant explosion alone is worth hunting down a nursery that can get you a yuzu tree.

fragrant orange-vanilla muesli

SERVES 4 TO 6

During an epic ninety-five-recipe shoot with a client, we were flooded with back-to-back dishes to photo-graph, but thanks to an incredibly organized team of chefs, we were able to flow through the shots very easily—that is, until the muesli dish came out to the shooting table. All of a sudden, the shoot came to a halt. We asked to have a taste of the muesli, and it was so good that the shoot was stalled until we had fin-ished the whole bowl. We had forgotten how much we love muesli, a dish made of uncooked oats soaked in milk, yogurt, or juice and then topped with fruit or nuts. Muesli stands as one of our favorite breakfasts. Our inspired version here is soaked in fresh orange juice and topped with fresh orange slices and a heaping serving of nuts and fruit. We call it our Mighty Muesli.

INGREDIENTS

2 cups (180g) old-fashioned oats

¼ cup (45g) dried cherries

¼ cup (48g) dried apricots, cut into pea-size pieces

1 cup (240ml) fresh orange juice

1 cup (240ml) milk

½ cup (120ml) yogurt

¼ cup (60ml) honey, preferably orange blossom

½ tablespoon vanilla extract

½ cup (60g) roughly chopped pistachios

1 tablespoon brown sugar

2 to 3 oranges

DIRECTIONS

1 In a bowl, combine the oats, cherries, and apricots. In a separate bowl, mix together the orange juice, milk, yogurt, honey, and vanilla extract. Add the liquid mix-ture to the oat mixture and stir to combine. Cover and refrigerate for 8 hours or overnight.

2 In a small bowl, combine the pistachios and brown sugar and set aside.

3 Slice the oranges into segments: Cut off the top and bottom of each orange down to the pulp. Standing the orange up on the cut end, slice off the remaining peel and pith. Cradling the orange in your hand, carefully slice along each side of the dividing membranes to cut out the segments.

4 To serve, spoon the muesli into bowls. Top with the pistachio mixture and the orange segments.

blood orange bars
with a brown butter crust

MAKES 12 (3-BY-4-INCH / 7.5-BY-10-CM) BARS

The recipe is enough to make the bars in a quarter-sheet pan, however, we know for most, blood oranges can be a bit expensive so a reduced recipe may be a better option. The recipe works perfect if you halve it and make the bars in a four-by-fourteen-inch tart pan (that is what was used in the photos) or use individual three- or four-inch tart pans. Or you can always substitute in some tangerine juice for the blood orange juice. The color will pale more toward the orange side, but it will still be delicious. Promise. Also, make sure to taste the sweetness of the curd as you are making it. Blood oranges can vary quite a bit on their sweetness, so adjust the sugar quantities to your desired taste.

INGREDIENTS

FOR THE BROWN BUTTER CRUST

½ pound (225g) unsalted butter

½ cup (100g) sugar

3 cups (375g) all-purpose flour

½ teaspoon sea salt or kosher salt

FOR THE BLOOD ORANGE CURD

¼ cup (30g) cornstarch

1½ cups (300g) sugar

1 teaspoon sea salt or kosher salt

12 eggs, beaten

4 egg yolks, beaten

Zest of 6 blood oranges

2½ cups (600ml) fresh blood orange juice

½ pound (225g) cold, unsalted butter, cut into ½-inch (12-mm) pieces

DIRECTIONS

1 Preheat the oven to 350°F (175°C).

2 **Make the brown butter crust:** In a saucepan, melt the butter over medium heat. The butter will foam up initially but then settle down. Continue cooking, swirling the pan occasionally, until the solids begin to separate and brown and the liquids turn a light brown color. The browned butter should have a nutty, toasty aroma. Remove the pan from the heat and stir in the sugar until mostly dissolved.

3 Put flour and salt in a large bowl. Stir in the butter and sugar mixture and mix until completely incorporated (the mixture will have a crumbly texture). Press the mixture into the bottom and sides of a rimmed 9-by-13-inch (23-by-33-cm) sheet pan.

4 Bake for about 30 minutes, or until the crust is golden.

5 **Make the blood orange curd:** Bring a pot of water to a gentle boil and place a heatproof bowl over the saucepan to make a double boiler.

recipe continues

6 In a bowl, whisk together the cornstarch, sugar, and salt. Mix in the eggs, egg yolks, blood orange zest, and blood orange juice. Place the mixture in the bowl of the double boiler and cook, stirring frequently, until the curd has thickened, about 8 minutes. Remove from the heat. Stir in the butter a few pieces at a time until it is completely incorporated. Strain the curd through a fine-mesh strainer into a bowl.

7 As soon as you take the crust out of the oven, pour the blood orange curd on top of it. Return the pan to the oven and bake for another 15 minutes, or until the filling has thickened. Remove from the oven and set aside to cool. When cool, place in the fridge to chill for at least 4 hours, preferably overnight.

8 Cut into bars and serve chilled.

meyer lemon-iced brown butter madeleines

MAKES 30 MINI MADELEINES

From Todd Madeleines will always have a special place in my heart. While working in the restaurant industry, my close friend Antoine and I would regain our afternoon sanity through a daily ritual during which we would pause and savor an espresso and a madeleine. The elegant simplicity of the madeleine and espresso combined with a dear friendship was always a life moment to bask in. The browned butter is a classic addition and imparts a wonderful nutty flavor to these delicate cookies. And finishing the madeleines with bright, floral Meyer lemon icing makes these irresistible to me.

INGREDIENTS

FOR THE MADELEINES

½ cup (1 stick / 113g) unsalted butter

1 tablespoon honey

1 cup (125g) flour

½ teaspoon baking powder

Finely grated zest of 1 Meyer lemon

2 eggs

⅔ cup (75g) confectioners' sugar

1 tablespoon brown sugar

Heavy pinch of kosher or sea salt

Melted butter, for brushing the molds

Flour, for dusting the molds

FOR THE MEYER LEMON ICING

½ tablespoon finely grated Meyer lemon zest

¼ cup (60ml) fresh Meyer lemon juice

⅛ teaspoon kosher or sea salt

3 tablespoons unsalted butter, melted

2½ cups (300g) confectioners' sugar

DIRECTIONS

1 **Make the madeleines:** In a saucepan, melt the butter over medium heat. The butter will foam up initially but then settle down. Continue cooking, swirling the pan occasionally, until the solids begin to separate and brown and the liquids turn a light brown color. The browned butter should have a nutty, toasty aroma. Remove the pan from the heat.

2 Stir the honey into the browned butter. Set aside and allow to cool a bit.

3 In a bowl, whisk together the flour, baking powder, and Meyer lemon zest for 20 seconds and then set aside.

4 In the bowl of a stand mixer fitted with the whisk attachment, whisk the eggs, confectioners' sugar, brown sugar, and salt together until pale yellow and at least doubled in volume. The batter should fall in ribbons from the whisk. (You can do this step by hand, but it takes a bit of whisking and is more comfortable to do with a mixer.)

5 Gently fold the flour mixture into the batter with a rubber spatula. Some flour streaks will still remain. Do not overmix.

recipe continues

6 Pour the cooled brown butter along the edge of the bowl so it gently pools on top of the batter. Gently fold it into the batter, trying to maintain the batter's volume as much as possible. Cover and refrigerate for 1 hour.

7 Preheat the oven to 425° F (220°C). Brush a mini-madeleine mold with melted butter, and then dust with flour. Tap out the excess flour.

8 Carefully pour the batter into a pastry bag fitted with a 4pt or 6pt tip (depending on your madeleine pan). (Alternatively, put the batter in a gallon-size zip-top bag and cut the tip off one corner.) Try to keep from overhandling and deflating the batter. Pipe batter into each cavity of the mold, filling each about 85 percent full (the batter will expand during baking, so don't worry about pressing it to the edges).

9 Place in the oven on the middle rack, and bake for no more than 5 minutes. (If you are using a regular-size madeleine pan, bake for no more than 10 minutes.) Be careful not to overbake the madeleines or they will dry out. Immediately remove the madeleines from the molds and place them on a wire rack.

10 **Make the icing:** In the clean bowl of a stand mixer fitted with the whisk attachment, whisk together the icing ingredients until smooth.

11 Dip the madeleines halfway into the icing, tap off any excess icing, then place them back on a wire rack until the icing cools. The madeleines are best served the same day.

homemade orange-tangerine soda

SERVES 4 TO 6

With any citrus that we can get our hands on, we'll whip up a batch of homemade soda. The possibilities are endless, and our fifteen citrus trees provide us with plenty of inspiration. Sodas made from the fresh juice and zest of mandarins, oro blancos, grapefruits, Meyer lemons, and oranges keep us hydrated all year long. Mixing citrus flavors together is another fun option for homemade soda, and if you've never made soda at home, you must try it once in this lifetime. The combination here of oranges and tangerines is a great way to start your own soda mixology. Best of all, you can control the amount of sugar in your own mix and make your soda less sweet and extra tart if you like. Before you know it, you'll be making pitchers of it and you'll say good-bye to the canned stuff. Trust us on this one!

INGREDIENTS

1 cup (240ml) fresh orange juice

1 cup (240ml) fresh tangerine juice

2 tablespoons Simple syrup (page 74), or to taste

12 ounces soda water

Ice

Wedges of fresh tangerines or oranges, for garnish

DIRECTIONS

1 In a large pitcher, combine the orange juice, tangerine juice, and simple syrup and mix well.

2 Gently stir in the soda water.

3 Serve in ice-filled glasses, garnished with citrus wedges.

classic bourbon sour with orange bitters

MAKES 1 COCKTAIL

The pivotal ingredient in a superb whiskey sour is the lemon and, accordingly, we planted a second lemon tree just for this cocktail. Fresh lemons have incredibly flavorful oils in their rind that quickly disappear as the lemons age after being picked. But when you're able to capture them fresh, the flavors of a seemingly everyday lemon are quite extraordinary. Orange bitters give another layer of flavor to this classic cocktail. Make your own bitters or find a store-bought favorite to keep on hand. The book *Bitters: A Spirited History of a Classic Cure-All* by Brad Thomas Parsons is a great resource for making your own bitters. We make a home-made tangerine bitters based off of Brad's orange bitters recipe, and it is perfect for cocktails like this one.

INGREDIENTS

Lemon wedge (optional)

Superfine sugar (optional)

Ice

1½ ounces bourbon

¾ ounce fresh lemon juice

¾ ounce Simple Syrup
(page 74)

A few dashes orange bitters

DIRECTIONS

1 If desired, rub the rim of a chilled cocktail glass with a lemon wedge and sugar the rim, or add ice cubes to a glass of your choice.

2 In a cocktail shaker filled with ice, combine the bourbon, lemon juice, simple syrup, and orange bitters. Shake vigorously for 15 to 20 seconds.

3 Strain into the chilled cocktail glass, or pour into the glass with ice, and serve.

lemon and cream spaghetti

SERVES 4 TO 6

When we dine in New York, our dear friend Jennifer Perillo is our trusted guide to some of the most incredible Italian food in the city. During one dinner at a restaurant, she introduced us to the most simple yet wonderful spaghetti dishes we've ever tasted. We embarrassed ourselves by inhaling one of the dishes so fast you'd think we'd never eaten pasta before: perfectly cooked spaghetti laced with bright, floral notes of lemon and prepared in a light cream sauce. From the first to the very last bite, we marveled at how such a simple dish could be so unforgettably delicious. We've created our own version so that we can enjoy it at home. With four lemon trees in our garden, we're always prepared to indulge in this beloved pasta dish.

INGREDIENTS

½ pound (225g) dry spaghetti

2 tablespoons olive oil

2 tablespoons heavy cream

½ cup (120ml) dry white wine

1 tablespoon fresh lemon zest, or more to taste

2 tablespoons fresh lemon juice, or more to taste

½ cup (50g) freshly grated Parmigiano Reggiano, or more to taste, plus extra for serving

DIRECTIONS

1 Fill a large pot with water, salt it well, and bring the water to a boil. Cook the spaghetti according to the package directions, or until al dente.

2 When the pasta is halfway cooked, begin making the sauce: In a saute pan large enough to later hold the pasta, whisk together the oil, cream, and wine. Over medium-high heat, bring the mixture to a simmer and cook for 2 to 3 minutes, whisking occasionally.

3 Drain the pasta and add it to the sauté pan. Add the lemon zest, lemon juice, and cheese and toss well. Taste for seasoning and add a touch more lemon or cheese, if desired.

4 Serve on warm plates with additional cheese on the side.

tangerine crème brûlée

MAKES TEN 4-OUNCE SERVINGS

Our Fremont tangerine tree was a skinny, runty-looking tree when we brought it home more than fifteen years ago. We nurtured it, planted it in the best location of the sun-filled garden, and did all we could to keep our Rhodesian Ridgeback from trampling it for the first two years. It wasn't, however, as healthy as we'd hoped. Then all of a sudden, after the second year, it seemed to hit a sweet spot in the soil and had a growth spurt to incredible heights. Our little "Charlie Brown" citrus tree exploded with fruit in huge, grape-like clusters. We couldn't believe how strong it became overnight, and after all these years it continues to give us juicy fruit that feeds our community of friends and neighbors. Motto of this story: Never, ever give up on your little trees because you never know how beautiful they can grow up to be. We're such proud parents. This recipe is to celebrate our once-wee-little tangerine tree.

INGREDIENTS

2½ cups (600ml) heavy cream

Finely grated zest of 6 medium tangerines

3 eggs

5 egg yolks

¾ cup (165g) packed brown sugar

½ cup (120ml) fresh tangerine juice

½ teaspoon salt

1 teaspoon vanilla extract

DIRECTIONS

1 Preheat the oven to 350°F (175°C). Place ten 4-ounce ceramic ramekins in a roasting pan or other suitable ovenproof dish taller than the ramekins. Add hot water to the pan until it reaches about three-quarters of the way up the sides of the ramekins. Remove the ramekins from the water and place the roasting pan in the oven (make sure there is no rack directly above it, so you'll have room to return the filled ramekins to the pan). Set the ramekins aside.

2 In a saucepan, combine the cream and tangerine zest. Over medium heat, warm the cream to the scalding point, stirring occasionally.

3 In a medium bowl, lightly whisk together the eggs and egg yolks. Whisk in ½ cup (110g) of the brown sugar and the tangerine juice.

4 Pour the egg mixture into the cream, stirring constantly. Add the salt and vanilla extract. Strain the custard through a fine-mesh sieve into a container that is easy to pour out of.

recipe continues

5 Divide the custard evenly among the ramekins; each one should be about three-quarters full. Open the oven door and carefully place the filled ramekins in the hot water bath.

6 Bake the custards for 25 to 30 minutes, or until they are just set (make sure not to overcook them—better under than over). Remove the ramekins from the water bath and place them on a kitchen towel (canning jar lifters work great for this step). Allow the custards to cool for about 20 minutes, then refrigerate them until they are thoroughly chilled. (The custards will keep for up to 5 days in the refrigerator; keep them well covered to prevent other smells from permeating them.)

7 Reduce the oven temperature to 300°F (150C°). Line a sheet pan with parchment paper.

8 Spread the remaining ¼ cup (55g) brown sugar into an even, thin layer on the sheet pan. Bake until the sugar starts to dry out (about 5 minutes). Remove from the oven, allow to cool, then roll the sugar with a rolling pin to break it up into granules again. Set aside in an airtight container until you are ready to serve the crème brûlées.

9 Sprinkle the brown sugar in a thin, even layer on the tops of the custards. Pass a kitchen torch over the custards with quick swirling motions until the sugar melts and burns slightly.

oro blanco and watercress salad

SERVES 4

Have you had an oro blanco yet? If not, you're in for a wonderful surprise. They're a cross between a white grapefruit and a pomelo, and when ripe, oro blancos range in color from green to yellow.

Oro blancos are sweet, floral, and less acidic than their regular grapefruit counterparts, which makes them perfect for a refreshing salad. If you can't find oro blancos, this salad works just as well with a sweet ruby red or star ruby grapefruit.

Beginning in late December, oro blancos come into season, and it's not uncommon for us to eat two or three in one sitting. Yes, we're that obsessed with them, and sadly our small oro blanco tree can't keep up with our ravenous appetites. Time to grow a second tree!

INGREDIENTS

2 medium oro blancos or grapefruits

1 tablespoon olive oil

½ tablespoon apple cider vinegar

¼ teaspoon kosher or sea salt

¼ teaspoon Dijon mustard

½ teaspoon brown sugar

1 bunch watercress, tough stems removed

¼ cup (35g) marcona almonds (or other nuts)

¼ cup (25g) freshly grated Parmesan

Freshly cracked black pepper

DIRECTIONS

1 Slice off the bottom of the oro blancos or grapefruits and stand them on the cut end. With a sharp knife, cut along the flesh of the fruit, removing the skin and white pith. Suprême the fruit by cutting along both sides of the membranes separating each segment. Set the segmented fruit wedges aside in a small bowl.

2 In a bowl, combine the oil, vinegar, salt, mustard, and brown sugar. Mix thoroughly.

3 In a large bowl, toss the fruit wedges with the watercress and vinegar mixture.

4 Divide the salad among 4 serving bowls or plates. Top each with a small handful of the nuts, the Parmesan, and pepper to taste.

kumquat marmalade

MAKES ABOUT 1½ CUPS (360ML)

Our once tiny kumquat tree isn't so tiny anymore. It's actually more than four feet tall now, which is huge compared to its gangly size when we brought it home. It grows slowly in our front yard, but every year it feeds us with enough adorable kumquats to make a great batch of marmalade. This is a marmalade recipe that we savor slowly during the season because the flavor of the rinds is so delicious and concentrated.

This recipe is based on a kumquat-to-sugar ratio of 1:¾. You can easily adjust proportionally if you want to make larger or smaller batches. The seeds provide the pectin for you, so make sure you don't throw them out when you're squeezing the kumquats.

INGREDIENTS

1 pound (455g) kumquats

¾ pound (340g) sugar (about 1⅔ cups)

DIRECTIONS

DAY 1

1 Slice the kumquats in half lengthwise. Over a bowl covered with a mesh strainer, squeeze the kumquats and rub them back and forth between your fingers. This will help loosen the fruit segments from the rinds. Remove the segments from the rinds and set both aside.

2 Wrap the segments and the seeds from the mesh strainers in cheesecloth. Slice the rinds into thin strips. In a large bowl, combine the cheesecloth bundle, the rinds, and the juice and add 2 cups (480ml) water to the bowl. Cover and set aside in the refrigerator for at least 12 hours to help soften the rinds.

DAY 2

1 Put five metal spoons in the freezer for testing the marmalade at the end of the cooking process. Set aside 3 sterilized 4-ounce glass jars (see Note, page 54).

2 Place the contents of the bowl (liquid, rinds, and cheesecloth bundle from the day before) in a medium saucepan. Add the sugar.

3 Over high heat, bring the mixture to a boil. Reduce the heat to medium and boil for at least 45

minutes before testing for doneness. (Do not stir during the initial bubbling, but after 10 minutes, stir occasionally to prevent the marmalade from burning.)

4 **Test the marmalade:** Remove the marmalade from the heat and put half a spoonful in one of the frozen spoons. Put the spoon back in the freezer for 3 minutes. Then remove the spoon from the freezer and test it. If the bottom of the spoon is still warm, continue freezing for another minute or so. Tip the spoon to see if the marmalade runs. If the top layer has set to a jelly consistency, the marmalade is done. If it runs, continue cooking for another few minutes and test again.

5 When the marmalade is done, remove the cheesecloth bundle and squeeze out any remaining liquid. Using a stainless-steel spoon, skim off any surface foam. Let the marmalade rest for 10 minutes, then pour it into remaining jars and follow the canning instructions on page 59.

yuzu kosho

MAKES ABOUT ⅓ CUP (80ML)

Yuzu is a Japanese citrus fruit valued for its highly aromatic rind. It is reminiscent of a classic Eureka lemon, an oro blanco grapefruit, and a lime but still has its own unique fragrance and flavor: a little floral, a little sour, and utterly wonderful. There isn't much juice on the interior, mostly seed, but the zest is intensely fragrant, and this is one of the few citrus fruits that don't diminish in flavor when cooked. In the garden, yuzu is one of the hardiest citrus plants; they are cold-resistant at temperatures as low as 5°F (−15°C). Just watch out for those thorns—they are deadly huge!

Hailing from the island of Kyushu in Japan, yuzu kosho is an amazing ingredient to have in the kitchen: bright, floral zest from yuzu fruit combined with chilies and salt. It has an intense pop of flavor and you'll often use just a touch of it: a dab in ramen or chicken soup, added to some soy sauce for a zesty dipping sauce, or rubbed on chicken or fish for grilling. You may find yourself addicted and start adding it into salads, appetizers, soups, main courses, and snacks.

Although yuzu can be hard to find, don't despair. You can create a similar condiment using lime, grapefruit, lemon, or a combination, with each providing its own unique personality. Yuzu kosho is traditionally made with a chile similar to Thai Bird's Eye chilies; but serranos or jalapeños are great variations if you can't get Thai chilies. Not having any Thai chilies in our garden, we developed this recipe with serranos.

Ingredient amounts are mere guidelines because chile spice levels and the intensity of the yuzu will vary. Find a ratio you like between the chile and yuzu, then add 10 percent of their combined weight in a good sea salt or kosher salt. (For example, if the minced chilies and yuzu zest weigh 100 grams, add 10 grams of salt.) When you taste the yuzu kosho, the citrus and salt will be the first things you notice on the tongue; then in a second or two you'll notice a nice fiery tingle. It is best to use gloves while making the yuzu kosho because you'll be getting intimate with those chilies.

INGREDIENTS

2 tablespoons (35g) finely grated yuzu zest (from 6 to 8 yuzu)

6 tablespoons (65g) stemmed, seeded, and finely minced serrano chilies (5 to 7 chilies)

Scant 2 teaspoons sea salt or kosher salt

DIRECTIONS

1 In a mortar and pestle or a food processor, combine the ingredients and grind them to a paste. Taste and adjust for desired flavor and spiciness.

2 Allow the yuzu kosho to cure in the fridge for 1 week. Store in an airtight container in the fridge for up to 1 month, or store batches in the freezer for up to 1 year.

stone fruits

HOW CAN ONE EVER FORGET BITING INTO A peach so juicy you have to suck in as you bite just to keep it from flowing down your chin? Stone fruits at the height of their seasons—plump peaches and nectarines, delicate apricots, crisp cherries, tart-skinned and sweet-fleshed plums—lead one to rhapsodize and swoon. And some recent additions to the food world—incredible hybrids such as pluots, plumcots, apruims, and nectaplums—all combine the best trait of one stone fruit with a complementary aspect of another.

Our love of stone fruits begins long before their summertime sweetness arrives. It starts in the spring, when their flowers break our garden's winter doldrums. We'll sense it coming in the subtle swelling of the buds just waiting for the first warmth of the season. Finally, for several days in a row the air will warm, and then one, two, three buds will appear. Suddenly the tree will begin to open up, its petals stretching out after a long winter's sleep. Within a week the tree will be filled with blossoms, signaling the arrival of spring.

As much pleasure as we derive from stone fruits, it seems as if their season is too short. In a mere few weeks many of the varieties in the local markets will turn from stellar to disappointing. Last week's sweet apricot is now mealy and lifeless. Fortunately each fading family is succeeded by some of its stone-fruit brethren that are just beginning to reach their prime. And even past their zenith, many stone fruits are still wonderful in the kitchen. Their sweetness and juicy texture may be lost when eaten out of hand, but the fruits can be given a new and delicious life when gently cooked.

Some varieties will last longer than others, but all in all their glory leaves us too soon. Another reminder to savor life—and its peaches—when Nature offers it.

roasted pluots with brown sugar and balsamic vinegar

SERVES 4

Though still in its young stage, our little pluot tree produces about six fruits a year, all of which are treasured like gold. We guard this tree fiercely because if we didn't, the squirrels would feast on all the fruit. They still haven't learned to share.

Roasted pluots are lusciously juicy and fragrant. Their sweet, meaty flesh, with its hints of balsamic vinegar, pairs nicely with both sweet and savory dishes. This recipe is so versatile that you can serve it with your favorite ice cream, yogurt, or grilled meat dishes—the possibilities are endless. And of course if you can't find pluots, sweet plums work equally well.

INGREDIENTS

2 tablespoons brown sugar

2 tablespoons olive oil

1 tablespoon balsamic vinegar

A few sprigs fresh thyme

1 pound (455g) ripe pluots (plum-apricot hybrids), halved, stones removed

DIRECTIONS

1 Preheat the oven to 350°F (175°C).

2 In a large bowl, combine the brown sugar, oil, vinegar, and thyme sprigs. Combine well.

3 Add the pluots to the mixture and gently mix.

4 Place the pluots, cut side up, on a baking dish.

5 Roast for 15 to 25 minutes, or until soft. (Less ripe pluots may take longer to cook.)

6 Allow to cool for 5 to 10 minutes, then serve warm.

brown sugar apricots
with vanilla rum ice cream

SERVES 4

Silky, velvety apricots are one of the first signs that summer has arrived. If we can't keep up with the delicate fruits, we'll cook them and serve them à la mode. There's always a tub of homemade ice cream in our fridge, and we love inventing flavors for every new batch. But a go-to favorite is our vanilla rum ice cream, which can be paired with almost any poached fruit. When apricots are peaking, a few tubs of vanilla rum ice cream will be ready and waiting in the freezer. These two are a perfect pair, a food match made in heaven.

Be careful when cooking the apricots, for two reasons. The brown sugar will be caramelized and very hot, and few things are worse than a caramel burn. Also, the apricots will soften from perfect to mushy very quickly. Cooking time will vary depending on their ripeness, so watch them closely after flipping them. This is also a great use for off-season apricots that no longer have the best texture and flavor.

INGREDIENTS

3 tablespoons unsalted butter

3 tablespoons brown sugar

¼ teaspoon ground cardamom

1 pound (455g) apricots, halved, stones removed

Vanilla Rum Ice Cream (recipe follows)

DIRECTIONS

1 In a large sauté pan, combine the butter, brown sugar, and cardamom over medium-high heat. Cook, stirring constantly, until the butter is melted.

2 Add the apricots, cut side down, and cook for 3 minutes. Carefully flip the apricots over and cook for 1 minute, or until they are soft but still holding their shape.

3 Remove from the heat and serve warm with vanilla rum ice cream.

VANILLA RUM ICE CREAM

MAKES ABOUT 1 QUART (1L)

INGREDIENTS

1½ cups (360ml) heavy cream

1 cup (240ml) milk

½ cup (100g) sugar

Pinch of kosher or sea salt

1 whole vanilla bean

5 egg yolks

1 teaspoon vanilla extract

2 tablespoons dark rum

SPECIAL EQUIPMENT
Ice cream machine

DIRECTIONS

1 In a medium saucepan, combine the cream, milk, sugar, and salt. Split the vanilla bean and scrape the seeds into the cream mixture, then add the bean pod as well.

2 Heat to a bare simmer over medium heat, stirring frequently. Remove from the heat and cover. Set aside for 30 minutes.

3 In a medium bowl, whisk the egg yolks. Slowly whisk the cream mixture into the yolks, then pour everything back into the saucepan.

4 Heat the mixture over medium heat, stirring constantly and scraping the bottom as you stir. Cook until the mixture thickens enough to coat the back of a spatula or wooden spoon, 1 to 2 minutes after reaching a bare simmer. Remove the vanilla bean pod.

5 Pour the custard through a fine-mesh strainer into a clean container. Place the container in an ice bath and stir the custard occasionally until it is cool, about 20 minutes.

6 Stir in the vanilla extract and rum. Cover and refrigerate for at least 2 hours or overnight.

7 Freeze according to the ice cream machine directions. While churning the ice cream, place the container in which you will store the ice cream in the freezer to chill. Store the ice cream in the freezer until ready to serve.

sautéed peaches with brown-butter pancakes

SERVES 4

Sweet peaches gently softened and glazed with brown sugar and cinnamon, nestled on top of fluffy pancakes—does a summer morning get any better? When you can't keep up with the abundance of peak peach season, treat yourself to this hearty breakfast that's equally suitable for dinner—yes, pancakes for dinner is definitely allowed!

Make sure not to overmix the batter, or the pancakes may come out dense and tough. If you want to keep the morning simple, you can always just melt the butter rather than browning it, but browning the butter gives the pancakes an extra dimension of flavor. But we do understand—sometimes the less we have to do in the morning the better, especially before that first cup of coffee.

INGREDIENTS

FOR THE TOPPING

2 tablespoons unsalted butter

2 tablespoons brown sugar

1 teaspoon ground cinnamon

4 medium peaches, ripe but firm, sliced into ½-inch (12-mm) wedges

FOR THE PANCAKES

2 cups (250g) flour

2 tablespoons brown sugar

2 teaspoons baking powder

1 teaspoon baking soda

1 teaspoon coarse kosher salt or sea salt

Dash of freshly grated nutmeg

¼ cup (½ stick / 55g) unsalted butter

2 cups (480ml) buttermilk (see Note, page 264)

2 eggs

Finely grated zest of 1 medium orange (optional)

Vegetable oil or nonstick cooking spray, for the skillet

DIRECTIONS

1 Make the topping: In a large sauté pan, melt the butter over medium-low heat. Add the brown sugar and cinnamon and stir to mix evenly. Add the peaches. Cook for just under 1 minute, then gently flip the peaches. Cook for another 30 seconds and remove from the heat. Set aside.

2 Make the pancakes: In a large bowl, combine the flour, brown sugar, baking powder, baking soda, salt, and nutmeg. Whisk for 20 seconds to thoroughly combine.

3 In a small saucepan, melt the butter over medium-high heat. Continue cooking until the butter starts to develop an amber color and gives off a nutty smell (if it seems like it is cooking too fast, occasionally lift the pan off the heat and give it a few swirls, then return it to the heat). Set aside.

4 If making your own buttermilk, prepare it now (see Note, page 264).

5 Place the buttermilk in a medium bowl. Whisk in the browned butter. Whisk in the eggs and the orange zest (if using).

recipe continues

NOTE To make buttermilk, for every 1 cup (240ml) milk, add 1 tablespoon lemon juice. Combine in a bowl, stir well, and set aside for 5 minutes before using as directed in the recipe.

6 Make a well in the dry ingredients. Pour the buttermilk mixture into the well. Combine the wet and dry ingredients by stirring from the center and gradually working your way out, just until there are no flour streaks (the batter will still be lumpy).

7 Heat a large pan or skillet over medium-high heat. Lightly brush the pan with a touch of oil or coat with nonstick cooking spray. In batches, ladle the batter into the pan to make pancakes. When the bottoms are golden and the tops are bubbly (1 to 2 minutes), flip the pancakes over and cook the second side until golden. Set the finished pancakes aside on a platter. Repeat until the batter is done.

8 Serve the pancakes topped with the glazed peaches and any other favorite toppings (maple syrup, whipped cream, butter . . .).

stone fruit parfait
with orange-vanilla granola

Summer wouldn't be the same without piles of ripe, juicy peaches, plums, or apricots in different corners of the kitchen and dining room. Oftentimes we'll add our favorite homemade granola and some yogurt to our stone fruit collection and dive into a hearty bowl of this breakfast parfait. This style of breakfast is also great for feeding a large group. With the three elements on the table, everyone can choose how to make their own parfait.

INGREDIENTS

FOR THE ORANGE-VANILLA GRANOLA

1 cup (120g) dried cranberries

4 cups (360g) old-fashioned rolled oats

1 cup (110g) raw chopped pecans

1 cup (140g) raw chopped cashews

½ cup (70g) raw sunflower seeds

¼ cup (½ stick / 57g) unsalted butter, melted

1 tablespoon vanilla extract

Finely grated zest of 2 large oranges

½ cup (120ml) fresh orange juice

1 teaspoon kosher or sea salt

½ cup (110g) brown sugar

½ cup (120ml) honey

Stone fruits, stones removed, cut into chunks

Plain or vanilla yogurt

DIRECTIONS

1 Preheat the oven to 300°F (150°C).

2 Soak the cranberries in hot water for 15 minutes. Drain the water, then combine all the granola ingredients in a large bowl and mix well. Spread the mixture evenly on a sheet pan.

3 Bake for about 1 hour, stirring every 15 minutes. Remove from the oven when the oats are golden. Set aside to cool.

4 Layer the granola, fruit, and yogurt together in bowls and serve.

peaches with sabayon and honey

SERVES 4

When peaches are sweet, dripping, and full of flavor, they are almost too good to cook. Sabayon is a perfect topping for these summertime treasures. It is a light, wine-infused mousse. The dry taste of Riesling pairs perfectly with the peaches, although it is also fun to experiment with other wines. There is a warm version and a cold version of the sabayon, the cold needing a bit of gelatin to stabilize it. Each style has its fans, but we're partial to the warm version.

INGREDIENTS

1 pound (455g) peaches (about 2 medium)

½ cup (120ml) dry Riesling wine

2 tablespoons sugar

8 egg yolks

2 pinches of unflavored gelatin (if making cold sabayon)

1 tablespoon honey

DIRECTIONS

Cut the peaches in half; remove the stones and any tough flesh in the cavity. Cut the peaches into ½-inch (12-mm) pieces and divide them among four serving glasses.

FOR WARM SABAYON

In a medium heatproof bowl, combine the wine, sugar, and egg yolks. Place the bowl over a pot of simmering water and whisk rapidly until the mixture just starts to hold its shape when you lift the whisk out of the bowl , about 4 minutes. Spoon the sabayon over the peaches and drizzle with honey.

FOR COLD SABAYON

1 In a medium heatproof bowl, combine the gelatin with 1 tablespoon of the wine and stir to dissolve. Whisk in the remaining wine and the sugar. Whisk in the egg yolks.

2 Place the bowl over a pot of simmering water and whisk rapidly until the mixture just starts to hold its shape when you lift the whisk out of the bowl, about 4 minutes.

3 Place the bowl in an ice bath and whisk slowly until cool. Place the bowl in the fridge until ready to serve.

4 Spoon the sabayon over the peaches and drizzle with honey.

cherry bourbon delight cocktail

MAKES 1 COCKTAIL

One of the drawbacks of living in Southern California is that many stone fruits don't grow very well here. Many of them require more chill hours than our temperate climate provides. It was a blow to our hopes when we realized that we wouldn't be able to grow our beloved cherries. A Southern California gardener's life is so rough! Although it does make us all the more excited when we start seeing cherries in our local markets. This muddling of cherries with bourbon and a little vermouth is a cocktail we created to celebrate the season of one of our favorite fruits.

INGREDIENTS

3 cherries, stemmed and pitted

Ice

½ ounce fresh lemon juice

½ ounce Simple Syrup (page 74)

½ ounce extra-dry vermouth

1 ounce bourbon

A few dashes Peychaud's Bitters, or bitters of your choosing

5 ounces soda water

DIRECTIONS

1 Muddle the cherries in a chilled glass.

2 In a shaker filled with ice, combine the lemon juice, simple syrup, vermouth, bourbon, and bitters and shake vigorously for 20 seconds.

3 Strain the cocktail over the cherries in the glass. Add ice and soda water. Stir gently and serve.

chocolate cherry crisp

SERVES 6

From Todd Diane loves cherries. She gets all gushy over them in ways that even I don't inspire in her. The first time we visited my dad together, it took her a whole five seconds to spot a random cherry tree growing in a ditch near Dad's ranch. Every time we visit, Diane immediately scopes the joint. Are the cherries ripe? Cherries have never been the same since teaming up with this little fruit burglar.

As with most fruit, our favorite way of enjoying cherries is to eat them immediately in their super-sweet state. Occasionally, however, we'll process the goods by baking them. What better way than with my all-time favorite country-style dessert, a crisp. This crisp has a perfect topping that conceals the ill-gotten gains beneath brown sugar, butter, flour, oats, and dark chocolate chips. This is an unforgettable treat.

INGREDIENTS

Butter, for the baking dish

FOR THE TOPPING

¾ cup (100g) flour

¼ cup (55g) packed brown sugar

½ tablespoon sea salt or kosher salt

½ cup (1 stick / 113g) cold unsalted butter, cut into small cubes

1 cup (90g) old-fashioned (not quick-cooking) rolled oats

FOR THE FILLING

2 pounds (910g) fresh cherries, pitted and halved

1 cup (180g) dark chocolate chips

¼ cup (50g) sugar

3 tablespoons flour

DIRECTIONS

1 Preheat the oven to 375°F (190°C). Butter a 2-quart (2-L) baking dish.

2 Make the topping: In a large bowl, mix together the flour, brown sugar, and salt. Pinching with your fingertips or using a pastry blender, work the butter into the flour mixture until it is the texture of coarse meal.

3 Add the oats, and use your hands to toss and squeeze the mixture until large, moist clumps form. Cover the mixture and transfer it to the freezer to chill while you prepare the filling.

4 Make the filling: If desired, set aside a handful of cherries to decorate the top of the crisp. In a large bowl, toss the cherries with the chocolate chips, sugar, and flour. Place the mixture in a baking dish and sprinkle with the topping. If desired, place the reserved cherries on top of the crisp.

5 Place the baking dish on a sheet pan and bake for 45 to 55 minutes, or until golden and bubbling. Let cool for 10 minutes before serving.

other tree & vine fruits

THIS IS THE EVERYTHING-ELSE CATEGORY, A special collection of fruits that we couldn't live without, yet couldn't find a better way to organize. Apples, pears, figs, pomegranates, persimmons, and melons are some of our beloved tree and vine fruits that explode during the latter part of the year. These are what we also call our transition fruits, because they straddle the seasons of summer and fall.

During our garden's first years, the pear and persimmon trees were quite a struggle to keep alive. Diseases and molds inhibited them from fruiting, always leaving sickly leaves and branches for us to use as study specimens. Keeping them healthy was always our primary goal, and if we were rewarded with fruit, we were beyond thrilled.

As we became more competent gardeners, the trees settled in. We protected their roots, became more consistent with watering, and fed the trees as if they were nursing mothers. We lost a couple of the weaker ones, but the lessons we learned helped us become better caretakers for the survivors. Now

they reward us, and all our garden's inhabitants, with their seasonal bounty.

The birds and squirrels in our garden would probably starve if it weren't for our family of tree and vine fruits. But rather than thanking us for nurturing these trees, the squirrels will chatter fiercely at us if we interrupt their morning feast of sweet figs or plump persimmons, and they'll scold Sierra and Lexi down below if the dogs are on fruit defense. From there, the squirrels will hop to the Asian pear trees to check on how ripe their fruits are for next week's dinner. Every morning is an ongoing chase between dogs who wish they could fly and chubby squirrels and birds who feel empowered because they're faster and smaller.

This battle for fruit between garden critters and dogs is constantly entertaining. And because of this, we don't mind sharing our tree and vine fruits, to keep the squirrels and birds happy throughout the year as well as for our own personal laughs.

butterscotch-apple mini galettes

MAKES 4 MINI GALETTES

Butterscotch: melted butter, caramelized sugars, cream, a little kick from the Scotch, and a touch of salt to round out the palate? Yeah, we swoon. We often use Fuji apples for these galettes, but feel free to use any of your favorite baking apples. This recipe can also be made into fewer but larger galettes; increase baking time slightly for larger sizes.

INGREDIENTS

FOR THE BUTTERSCOTCH
¼ cup (½ stick / 57g) unsalted butter

½ cup (110g) packed brown sugar

½ cup (100g) granulated sugar

½ cup (120ml) heavy cream

1 teaspoon vanilla extract

1 to 2 tablespoons Scotch or other whiskey

½ to ¾ teaspoon salt, or to taste

FOR THE FILLING
1½ pounds (680g) apples (3 to 4 medium), peeled, cored, and thinly sliced

¼ cup (50g) granulated sugar

1 tablespoon flour

1 tablespoon fresh lemon juice

ingredients continue

DIRECTIONS

1 **Make the butterscotch:** In a medium saucepan, melt the butter over medium-low heat. Just before it is completely melted, add both the sugars and stir. Gently cook, stirring occasionally, until the sugars transform from grainy to smooth (about 5 minutes).

2 While whisking, pour in the cream and continue whisking until homogenous. Increase the heat to medium and cook for 8 minutes, whisking occasionally.

3 Let cool for 10 minutes, then add the vanilla extract, whiskey, and salt. Set aside.

4 **Make the filling:** In a bowl, combine the filling ingredients. Toss to mix evenly and set aside.

5 Preheat the oven to 425°F (220°C). Line two sheet pans with parchment paper.

6 **Make the crust:** In a medium bowl, use your fingertips to pinch together the flour, butter, salt, and sugar until the mixture is crumbly and any large chunks of butter are flattened or broken up.

recipe continues

fig and gorgonzola pillows

MAKES 18 PILLOWS

Beginning in late summer, the battle for the garden figs begins. Our local squirrels and birds decide our fig tree is their favorite restaurant, but we also want to make sure we get our fair share. The pups do a valiant job of guarding, but there is only so much a canine can do against a tree dweller. It's always an amusing scene to see the pups wriggle and whine under the tree, clearly wishing they had wings.

Since we started making these fig and gorgonzola pillows, we've spent even more time on fig watch. Flaky, buttery puff pastry, figs, onion, gorgonzola, and often prosciutto all bake up together into an amazing savory-sweet treat. Good thing our fig tree keeps growing like a weed.

INGREDIENTS

1 tablespoon olive oil, plus more for drizzling

1 medium onion, sliced

3 pounds (1.4kg) Puff Pastry Dough (page 284)

Flour, for dusting work surface and dough

1 egg white

4 ounces (113g) prosciutto (optional)

6 ounces (170g) gorgonzola

14 to 16 fresh figs, cut into quarters

Freshly cracked black pepper

DIRECTIONS

1 Preheat the oven to 500°F (260°C). Line three sheet pans with parchment paper.

2 Heat a sauté pan over medium heat. Add the oil and onion, and cook, stirring occasionally, until the onions are soft, about 5 minutes. Set aside to cool.

3 Divide the puff pastry dough into three even sections, to make it easier to handle. Wrap two sections and place them in the fridge while you work with the first section.

4 On a lightly floured surface, roll the first section of dough out to a 12-by-18-inch (30-by-45-cm) rectangle, dusting the top and the bottom of the dough with flour as necessary.

5 Cut the dough into six 6-inch (15-cm) squares, using a ruler to mark the edges and help guide you.

6 Take one square and fold two diagonal corners to meet in the center. Repeat for the other two corners. Press to seal where the corners meet, and place the "pillow" on a lined sheet pan. Repeat with the other squares of dough.

recipe continues

7 In a small bowl, whisk together the egg white and 1 tablespoon water. Brush the pillows with the egg wash.

8 Place a scattering of onions on each pillow. Top with a small slice of prosciutto, if using. Pinch a few pieces of gorgonzola onto each pillow.

9 Add 2 or 3 fig quarters to each pillow. Add a bit of freshly cracked pepper to each pillow and drizzle the pillows with a little olive oil.

10 Repeat with the other two sections of dough, keeping the assembled pillows in the fridge until ready to bake.

11 Bake for 15 minutes (see Note), rotating the pans once after 10 minutes, until the puff pastry is golden.

NOTE Unless your oven capacity is very large, it is advisable to bake the pillows one sheet pan at a time to ensure even baking. If you have a good-size convection oven, you can bake them all at once, evenly spaced in the oven; just make sure to adjust cooking time as needed (the puff pastry may cook faster in a convection oven), and rotate the trays once during baking.

pear-dorf salad

SERVES 4

As an ode to one of our favorite fruits, we personalized a version of the classic Waldorf salad by using sweet seasonal pears. With so many pear varieties to choose from, it's always such a treat to welcome the autumn season by having a pear-centric salad. For glorious color, use red Anjou or Seckel pears for their beautiful skins. The wonderful balance of crunchy celery, sweet grapes, chewy raisins, and crisp pears is harmony in a bowl. Asian pears are also a great addition to this salad because of their crisp, juicy flesh. You can personalize this salad further with your own favorite pear variety.

INGREDIENTS

FOR THE DRESSING
¼ cup (60ml) mayonnaise
¼ cup (60ml) yogurt
½ teaspoon fresh lemon juice
¼ teaspoon kosher or sea salt
¼ teaspoon freshly cracked black pepper

FOR THE SALAD
2 ripe pears, chopped
½ cup (50g) chopped celery
½ cup (75g) grapes, halved
3 tablespoons golden raisins
⅓ cup (60g) chopped walnuts
2 cups (110g) chopped fresh lettuce

DIRECTIONS

1 **Make the dressing:** In a bowl, combine all the dressing ingredients. Mix well, and chill for about 20 minutes before serving.

2 **Make the salad:** In a large bowl, combine all the salad ingredients.

3 Before serving, add the dressing to the salad and toss well. Serve cold.

gin cocktail
with pomegranate and grapefruit

MAKES 1 COCKTAIL

One of the first times we saw a full-grown pomegranate tree was at a café where it was growing over an arbor. It was fall, and the beautiful red pomegranates were dangling through the trellis. It was hard to not be inspired by that scene. When hanging from their delicate branches in the fall, the fully ripe pomegranates open up and offer their seeds to the world. With this in mind, pomegranates were one of the first fruit trees we planted in our garden, trellising them over an archway that allowed the fruit to dangle within easy reach. It is one of our favorite autumn harvests. This drink muddles a small handful of ruby-red pomegranate seeds with fresh grapefruit juice and gin. Balanced with a bit of simple syrup and some orange bitters, it is a refreshing late-summer or fall cocktail.

INGREDIENTS

3 tablespoons pomegranate seeds

1½ ounces fresh grapefruit juice

1½ ounces gin

1 ounce Simple Syrup (page 74)

A few dashes orange bitters

Ice

DIRECTIONS

1 Muddle the pomegranate seeds in a cocktail shaker. Add the grapefruit juice, gin, simple syrup, bitters, and ice.

2 Shake vigorously for 15 to 20 seconds. Strain into a chilled cocktail glass.

fresh persimmon cookies with raisins and nuts

MAKES 24 COOKIES

Every year the persimmon tree branches bend to the ground from the weight of the heavy fruit they bear. When the persimmons peak with their deep orange colors, the whole tree looks like an autumn-decorated Christmas tree. This is also one of the trees that the birds enjoy feasting on. Their keen sense of smell allows them to always beat us to the ripest fruit on the tree. If we want to get to it first, we have to wake up early in the morning to pick the fruit that has ripened overnight. This is another of our favorite fruit desserts— it's very simple and makes great use of supersoft ripe persimmon flesh. These are gloriously soft, moist cookies; the recipe was passed on from Todd's grandmother's recipe cards. Cranberries would be an excellent substitute for the raisins, and chocolate chips are another great addition—both suggestions from Todd's mom.

INGREDIENTS

½ cup (1 stick / 113g) unsalted butter, at room temperature

1 cup (200g) sugar

1 egg

1 cup (240ml) fresh persimmon pulp

1 teaspoon baking soda

2 cups (250g) flour

½ teaspoon salt

½ teaspoon ground cinnamon

¼ teaspoon freshly grated nutmeg

¼ teaspoon ground cloves

1 cup (145g) raisins

1 cup (120g) chopped nuts

DIRECTIONS

1 Preheat the oven to 325°F (165°C). Line a sheet pan with parchment paper.

2 In a large bowl, cream together the butter and sugar until light and fluffy. Mix in the egg.

3 In a separate bowl, mix together the persimmon pulp and baking soda. Add to the butter mixture and stir to combine.

4 In another bowl, combine the flour, salt, cinnamon, nutmeg, and cloves and whisk for 20 seconds. Gently stir the dry ingredients into the wet ingredients. Stir in the raisins and nuts. Cover and refrigerate for at least 30 minutes. (Chilling the cookie dough at this point will result in fluffier cookies.)

5 Drop spoonfuls of the dough on the prepared sheet pan. Keep the cookies small and far apart, as they spread out while baking. Bake for 15 to 18 minutes, or until set and light golden around the edges.

homemade pineapple teriyaki sauce

MAKES ABOUT 2 CUPS (480ML)

When you make this, make plenty of it—you'll be surprised how fantastic a simple homemade teriyaki sauce can be. Made from fresh pineapple, this sauce has amazing flavor, without all the heavy sweeteners found in store-bought brands. So many people will be asking you for the recipe that you might as well give bottles of it as gifts—or make a few bucks by selling them to your neighbors!

We originally shared this recipe a few years on the blog, and we've used it in recipes here in the cookbook: Summer Squash Stuffed with Teriyaki Pork (page 164) and Sweet Pepper and Teriyaki Chicken Skewers (page 187). Think "outside the bottle" and add this sauce to all your barbecue and grilling recipes.

If you wish, add a little extra sugar for sweetness or vinegar for tang. Customize the teriyaki sauce to your taste!

INGREDIENTS

½ cup (120ml) soy sauce

1 cup (200g) minced fresh pineapple or canned crushed pineapple

1 (1-inch / 2.5-cm) knob ginger, minced

2 cloves garlic, minced

3 tablespoons brown sugar

1 teaspoon apple cider vinegar or rice vinegar

½ teaspoon sesame oil

1 tablespoon cornstarch

DIRECTIONS

1 In a blender, combine the soy sauce, pineapple, ginger, garlic, brown sugar, vinegar, and sesame oil. Puree until all the ingredients are well combined and the mixture is smooth.

2 In a small bowl, mix the cornstarch with 1 tablespoon cold water. With a fork, break apart the clumps until the liquid is smooth.

3 Transfer the pineapple mixture to a saucepan over medium-high heat. Bring to a boil and cook for about 1 minute. Immediately stir in the cornstarch slurry. Stir rapidly until the sauce thickens. Use a fork or whisk to smooth the sauce. Boil for about 1 minute, or until the sauce thickens. Remove from the heat and allow to cool.

honeydew salad
with riesling and mint

SERVES 4 TO 6

Even after a long meal with all the trimmings, we always have room left for dessert. When our bellies are bulging from a heavy meal, something simple, light, and refreshing helps the digestion process. Well, at least we've convinced ourselves that this is true! Generally, we lean toward desserts made with whatever fruits are peaking during that time of year. This refreshing pairing of our favorite summertime white wine with succulent honeydew and a touch of mint really hits the spot at the end of a great feast. Select a melon that is entering the very ripe stage. The sweet, juicy flesh will add extra flavor to the wine-and-mint base.

INGREDIENTS

1 small honeydew melon
  (4 to 5 pounds / 1.8 to 2kg),
  quartered and peeled

½ cup (120ml) Riesling or sweet
  white wine

3 tablespoons minced fresh mint
  leaves

DIRECTIONS

1 Cut the melon into bite-size pieces.

2 In a bowl, combine the melon, wine, and mint leaves and gently mix.

3 Chill for about 2 hours before serving.

fresh cantaloupe jam

MAKES ABOUT 2 CUPS (480ML)

We had a pleasant new experience during breakfast one morning in Mexico. While eating at a café, we were served a trio of homemade "fresh jams," made of minced papaya, kiwi, and cantaloupe. This concept of "jam" was surprisingly different, in that it consisted simply of finely minced fruit mixed with honey and a squeeze of lime. We spread the jam on some warm mini baguettes, and it was love at first bite. This version of jam highlights fresh fruit at its best, without all the sugar and thickeners—the fruit remains the hero. What a great way to start our mornings in Mexico, and now our mornings at home.

When mincing the cantaloupe, you'll have extra juice. Allow the excess juices to drain a bit so that your jam doesn't become too watery.

INGREDIENTS	DIRECTIONS
1 medium cantaloupe, peeled	1 Cut the cantaloupe in half and remove the seeds.
Zest of 1 lime	
2 teaspoons fresh lime juice	2 Mince the cantaloupe very fine. Place in a colander and allow all the juices to drain.
½ teaspoon honey	
	3 In a bowl, combine the cantaloupe, lime zest, lime juice, and honey.
	4 Chill for about 1 hour.

watermelon mojito

MAKES 1 COCKTAIL

We have a soft spot for mojitos, especially after traveling to Cuba, where they were a daily staple for our gang. While in Cuba, we soaked up the whole culture of mojitos, including how to make them. After finally getting a watermelon seedling to take off in our garden, we had a wheelbarrow full of the green-skinned, red-fleshed behemoths to play with, and we came up with this variation on the mojito. The trio of fresh watermelon, mint, and rum makes one of the most refreshing summer cocktails imaginable. It also works great by the pitcher for summertime gatherings: Muddle the watermelon and mint, then combine everything except the soda water in a pitcher. Serve over ice, with the soda water on the side.

INGREDIENTS

4 (1-inch / 2.5-cm) cubes watermelon (rind and seeds removed)

6 mint leaves, torn into small pieces

1 ounce fresh lime juice

1 ounce Simple Syrup (page 74)

1½ ounces light rum

Ice

4 ounces soda water

DIRECTIONS

1 In a small bowl or bartender's glass, muddle together the watermelon and mint leaves until the mixture reaches your preferred texture. Stir in the lime juice, simple syrup, and rum.

2 Place the ice in a highball glass and pour the mixture into the glass. Slowly add the soda water and gently mix.

melon sangria

Heirloom melons are an exciting new group of fruit to us, and we're starting to learn more about all the specialty varieties that are making waves at farmer's markets. Unique types like Ambrosia, Canary, and Charentais have a wide array of flavors, ranging from richly fruity to delicately floral. Eating melons fresh is absolutely our first choice—to bite into a thick, juicy wedge of melon is to taste nature's candy at its best. But if we come across a few extras, one always goes into a batch of fantastic melon sangria. The sweet succulence of melons infused for a few hours with white wine proves to be an outstanding beverage to share at gatherings. Summer just isn't the same without pitchers of melon sangria. This is our summer party drink of choice because we can prepare a few pitchers of it ahead of time and please a large crowd. So if you can score two ripe heirloom melons, designate one for eating and one for drinking. Celebrate summer!

INGREDIENTS

3 cups (480g) cubed fresh
heirloom melon

1 (750-ml) bottle dry white wine

3 tablespoons Simple Syrup
(page 74)

1 (750-ml) bottle soda water

DIRECTIONS

1 In a large pitcher, combine all the ingredients except the soda water.

2 Chill for 4 to 5 hours to allow the fruit to absorb the wine.

3 When ready to serve, add the soda water, gently stir, and serve.

index

almonds: Blueberry Frangipane
  Tarts, 229–30
  Creamed Haricots Verts with
  Toasted Almonds, 90
  Lettuce Wraps with Almond-
  Basil Chicken, 82
apples: Butterscotch-Apple Mini
  Galettes, 276–78
  Roasted Gold Nugget Squash
  with Apples and Brown Butter,
  168
  Warm Kale Salad with Apples
  and Dried Cranberries, 127
apricots: Stone Fruit Parfait with
  Orange-Vanilla Granola, 266
Artichokes, Braised, in White
  Wine, 104–5
arugula: Arugula with Braised
  Pork Shoulder, 132
  Grape, Arugula, and Brie
  Bruschetta, 279
  Pizza with Caramelized Fennel,
  Arugula, and Lemon, 154
asparagus: Asparagus and
  Cippolini Quiche, 101–3
  Roasted Asparagus Spring Rolls
  with Bacon, 107–8
  Smashed Cauliflower
  Sandwiches with Roasted
  Asparagus, 121
avocados: Chopped Kale Salad
  Massaged with Avocado, 128
  Spinach and Bacon Salad with
  Avocado Vinaigrette, 81

bacon: Butternut Squash Crumble,
  177
  Roasted Asparagus Spring Rolls
  with Bacon, 107–8
  Spinach and Bacon Salad with
  Avocado Vinaigrette, 81
Banh Mi, Grilled-Zucchini, 178
Barbecue Sauce from Fresh
  Tomatoes, 56
Barley, Charred Bell Peppers and
  Sausage with, 184
basil: Basil Pesto Farro Salad, 71
  Fresh Herb Pesto, 72
  Lettuce Wraps with Almond-
  Basil Chicken, 82
beans: Creamed Haricots Verts
  with Toasted Almonds, 90
  Tender Roasted Green Beans
  with Walnuts and Feta, 93
Beet Chips, Olive Oil–Baked, with
  Sea Salt and Black Pepper, 137
bell peppers. See peppers

berries, 219–33. See also
  blackberries
  Blueberry Frangipane Tarts,
  229–30
  Casanova Cocktail, 230
  Marionberry Mojito Ice Pops, 233
  Mixed Berry Chocolate Slab Pie,
  224–26
  Roasted-Strawberry Scones, 223
blackberries: Blackberry Cabernet
  Crisp with Honeyed Whipped
  Cream, 220–21
  Marionberry Mojito Ice Pops, 233
Blood Orange Bars with a Brown
  Butter Crust, 237–38
Blueberry Frangipane Tarts,
  229–30
Bourbon Sour with Orange Bitters,
  244
Bread Pudding, Rhubarb-Vanilla,
  109–10
breads. See also Bruschetta;
  sandwiches
  Herbed Garlic Knots, 64–66
breakfast: Baked Eggs in
  Tomatoes, 51
  Fragrant Orange-Vanilla
  Muesli, 236
  Roasted-Strawberry Scones, 223
  Sautéed Peaches with Brown-
  Butter Pancakes, 263–64
  Stone Fruit Parfait with Orange-
  Vanilla Granola, 266
Brie, Grape, and Arugula
  Bruschetta, 279
Broccoli and Grilled Cheese Melt,
  114
brown butter: Blood Orange Bars
  with a Brown Butter Crust,
  237–38
  Meyer Lemon–Iced Brown
  Butter Madeleines, 241–42
  Roasted Gold Nugget Squash
  with Apples and Brown Butter,
  168
  Sautéed Peaches with Brown-
  Butter Pancakes, 263–64
Brown Sugar Apricots with
  Vanilla Rum Ice Cream, 261–62
Bruschetta, Grape, Arugula, and
  Brie, 279
Brussels Sprouts, Braised, with
  Pancetta and Parmesan, 117
butter, 34
Butternut Squash Crumble, 177
Butterscotch-Apple Mini Galettes,
  276–78

cabbage: Grilled Cabbage Wedges,
  120
  Vietnamese Napa Cabbage
  Chicken Salad, 124
cakes: Meyer Lemon-Iced Brown
  Butter Madeleines, 241–42
  Zucchini-Cardamom Mini Tea
  Cakes, 171
Cantaloupe Jam, Fresh, 294
Cardamom-Zucchini Mini Tea
  Cakes, 171
carrots: Seared Ginger Carrots
  with Thyme and Shallots, 138
Casanova Cocktail, 230
cauliflower: Smashed Cauliflower
  Sandwiches with Roasted
  Asparagus, 121
  Spicy Roasted Cauliflower with
  Sriracha and Sesame, 118
celery: Pear-dorf Salad, 287
  Sautéed Celery and Shrimp, 94
  Celery Root and Red Lentil Soup,
  Hearty, 142
cheese. See also specific types
  Roasted Broccoli and Grilled
  Cheese Melt, 114
  Sweet Onion Crack Dip, 160
cherries: Cherry Bourbon Delight
  Cocktail, 270
  Chocolate Cherry Crisp, 273
chicken: Creamed Dill Chicken
  Potpie with Puff Pastry, 86–87
  Curried Kabocha Squash and
  Chicken Stew, 167
  Habanero Chicken Tacos, 194
  Jicama Chicken Cashew Salad
  with Mustard Dressing, 157
  Kale and Chicken Egg Rolls with
  Ginger Soy Dip, 129
  Lettuce Wraps with Almond-
  Basil Chicken, 82
  Sweet Pepper and Teriyaki
  Chicken Skewers, 187
  Vietnamese Napa Cabbage
  Chicken Salad, 124
chilies. See also salsa
  Blistered Shishito Peppers with
  Yuzu Kosho, 191
  Chile Margarita with Paprika
  Salt, 188
  Habanero Chicken Tacos, 194
  Yuzu Kosho, 255
chocolate: Chocolate Cherry Crisp,
  273
  Mixed Berry Chocolate Slab Pie,
  224–26
  Peppermint Chocolate Chip Ice
  Cream, 79–80

Sweet Potato and Chocolate Squares, 158–59
Cippolini and Asparagus Quiche, 101–3
cocktails. See drinks
Cookies, Fresh Persimmon, with Raisins and Nuts, 291
corn: Corn Fritters, 211
Roasted-Corn Tabouli, 200
Corriher, Shirley, 284
Crème Brûlée, Tangerine, 249–50
crisp: Blackberry Cabernet Crisp with Honeyed Whipped Cream, 220–21
Chocolate Cherry Crisp, 273
cucumbers: Cucumber Mint Quinoa Salad with Shallot Vinaigrette, 203
Miso-Sesame Cucumber Salad, 204
Curried Kabocha Squash and Chicken Stew, 167

Delicata Squash Rings, Roasted and Stuffed, 180
desserts. See cakes; ice cream; pies and pastries; sweets
Dill Chicken Potpie with Puff Pastry, 86–87
dips. See also salsa
Chunky Roasted Eggplant and Parmesan Dip, 208
Kale and Chicken Egg Rolls with Ginger Soy Dip, 129
Roasted Cherry Tomato and Goat Cheese Dip, 45
Sweet Onion Crack Dip, 160
Dried Cranberries, Warm Kale Salad with Apples and, 127
drinks: Casanova Cocktail, 230
Cherry Bourbon Delight Cocktail, 270
Chile Margarita with Paprika Salt, 188
Classic Bourbon Sour with Orange Bitters, 244
Gin Cocktail with Pomegranate and Grapefruit, 288
Homemade Orange-Tangerine Soda, 243
Melon Sangria, 298
Rosemary Lemonade, 74
Watermelon Mojito, 297

edamame: Crispy Soybean Fritters, 97
Egg Rolls, Kale and Chicken, with Ginger Soy Dip, 129
eggplants: Chunky Roasted Eggplant and Parmesan Dip, 208

Grilled Japanese Eggplants with Orange Zest and Sake Glaze, 207
eggs, 32
Baked Eggs in Tomatoes, 51
equipment, 35

Farro Salad with Basil Pesto, 71
Fennel, Caramelized, Pizza with Arugula, Lemon, and, 154
Feta, Tender Roasted Green Beans with Walnuts and, 93
Fig and Gorgonzola Pillows, 281–82
flour, 32
Frangipane Tarts, Blueberry, 229–30
fritters: Corn Fritters, 211
Crispy Soybean Fritters, 97
Italian-Style Fried Okra, 212

galettes: Butterscotch-Apple Mini Galettes, 276–78
Heirloom Tomato Galettes, 43–44
Garlic Knots, Herbed, 64–66
Garlic Soy Dipping Sauce, 108
Gin Cocktail with Pomegranate and Grapefruit, 288
ginger: Ginger Soy Dip, Kale and Chicken Egg Rolls with, 129
Red Tomato Jam with Fresh Ginger, 59
Seared Ginger Carrots with Thyme and Shallots, 138
goat cheese: Creamed Swiss Chard in Goat Cheese on Baked Potatoes, 85
Roasted Cherry Tomato and Goat Cheese Dip, 45
Gold Nugget Squash, Roasted, with Apples and Brown Butter, 168
Gorgonzola and Fig Pillows, 281–82
Granola, Orange-Vanilla, Stone Fruit Parfait with, 266
grapefruit: Gin Cocktail with Pomegranate and Grapefruit, 288
Oro Blanco and Watercress Salad, 251
grapes: Grape, Arugula, and Brie Bruschetta, 279
Pear-dorf Salad, 287
Green Tomato Pickles, Zesty, 55

Habanero Chicken Tacos, 194
Haricots Verts, Creamed, with Toasted Almonds, 90

Heirloom Tomato Galettes, 43–44
herbs, 63, 64–80. See also basil; mint; rosemary
Creamed Dill Chicken Potpie with Puff Pastry, 86–87
Fresh Herb Pesto, 72
Herb-Crusted Salmon, 67
Herb-Smashed Turnips with Parmesan, 147
Herbed Garlic Knots, 64–66
Mussels Steamed with Herbs and White Wine, 75
Honeydew Salad with Riesling and Mint, 293

ice cream: Peppermint Chocolate Chip Ice Cream, 79–80
Roasted-Pumpkin Ice Cream, 172
Vanilla Rum Ice Cream, 262
Ice Pops, Marionberry Mojito, 233
Italian-Style Fried Okra, 212

jams: Fresh Cantaloupe Jam, 294
Kumquat Marmalade, 252–53
Red Tomato Jam with Fresh Ginger, 59
Jicama Chicken Cashew Salad with Mustard Dressing, 157

Kabocha Squash and Chicken Stew, Curried, 167
kale: Chopped Kale Salad Massaged with Avocado, 128
Kale and Chicken Egg Rolls with Ginger Soy Dip, 129
Warm Kale Salad with Apples and Dried Cranberries, 127
Kumquat Marmalade, 252–53

lemons: Lemon and Cream Spaghetti, 247
Meyer Lemon–Iced Brown Butter Madeleines, 241–42
Pizza with Caramelized Fennel, Arugula, and Lemon, 154
Rosemary Lemonade, 74
lentils: Hearty Celery Root and Red Lentil Soup, 142
Lettuce Wraps with Almond-Basil Chicken, 82

Madeleines, Brown Butter, Meyer Lemon–Iced, 241–42
Margarita, Chile, with Paprika Salt, 188
Marionberry Mojito Ice Pops, 233
Marmalade, Kumquat, 252–53
melons: Fresh Cantaloupe Jam, 294
Honeydew Salad with Riesling and Mint, 293

Melon Sangria, 298
Watermelon Mojito, 297
Meyer Lemon–Iced Brown Butter
    Madeleines, 241–42
mint: Cucumber Mint Quinoa
    Salad with Shallot Vinaigrette,
    203
    Honeydew Salad with Riesling
    and Mint, 293
    Marionberry Mojito Ice Pops, 233
    Peppermint Chocolate Chip Ice
    Cream, 79–80
    Quick Pickled Sugar Snap Peas
    with Mint, 100
    Roasted-Corn Tabouli, 200
    Watermelon Mojito, 297
Miso-Sesame Cucumber Salad,
    204
Mizuna Mustard Salad, Wilted,
    with Shrimp, 131
Muesli, Fragrant Orange-Vanilla,
    236
Mussels Steamed with Herbs and
    White Wine, 75
Mustard Dressing, Jicama Chicken
    Cashew Salad with, 157
mustard greens: Wilted Mizuna
    Mustard Salad with Shrimp,
    131

Napa Cabbage Chicken Salad,
    Vietnamese, 124

oils, 34
Okra, Italian-Style Fried, 212
onions: Asparagus and Cippolini
    Quiche, 101–3
    Sweet Onion Crack Dip, 160
oranges: Blood Orange Bars with a
    Brown Butter Crust, 237–38
    Classic Bourbon Sour with
    Orange Bitters, 244
    Fragrant Orange-Vanilla
    Muesli, 236
    Grilled Japanese Eggplants with
    Orange Zest and Sake Glaze,
    207
    Homemade Orange-Tangerine
    Soda, 243
    Stone Fruit Parfait with Orange-
    Vanilla Granola, 266
Oro Blanco and Watercress Salad,
    251

Pancakes, Brown-Butter, Sautéed
    Peaches with, 263–64
pancetta: Braised Brussels Sprouts
    with Pancetta and Parmesan,
    117
    Butternut Squash Crumble, 177
pantry ingredients, 32–34

Paprika Salt, Chile Margarita
    with, 188
Parmesan cheese: Braised
    Brussels Sprouts with Pancetta
    and Parmesan, 117
    Chunky Roasted Eggplant and
    Parmesan Dip, 208
    Herb-Smashed Turnips with
    Parmesan, 147
    Sweet Onion Crack Dip, 160
Parsley Root, Roasted, with Red
    Quinoa, 141
pasta: Lemon and Cream
    Spaghetti, 247
    Picnic Pasta Salad with Roasted
    Tomato and Tuna, 54
Pea Sprout Spring Rolls, 108
peaches: Peaches with Sabayon
    and Honey, 269
    Sautéed Peaches with Brown-
    Butter Pancakes, 263–64
    Stone Fruit Parfait with Orange-
    Vanilla Granola, 266
Pear-dorf Salad, 287
peas: Quick Pickled Sugar Snap
    Peas with Mint, 100
Peppermint Chocolate Chip Ice
    Cream, 79–80
peppers: Charred Bell Peppers and
    Sausage with Pearled Barley,
    184
    Sweet Pepper and Teriyaki
    Chicken Skewers, 187
Persimmon Cookies with Raisins
    and Nuts, 291
pesto: Basil Pesto Farro Salad, 71
    Fresh Herb Pesto, 72
pickles: for Grilled-Zucchini Banh
    Mi, 178
    Quick Pickled Sugar Snap Peas
    with Mint, 100
    Zesty Green Tomato Pickles, 55
pies and pastries: Asparagus and
    Cippolini Quiche, 101–3
    Blood Orange Bars with a
    Brown Butter Crust, 237–38
    Blueberry Frangipane Tarts,
    229–30
    Butterscotch-Apple Mini
    Galettes, 276–78
    Creamed Dill Chicken Potpie
    with Puff Pastry, 86–87
    Fig and Gorgonzola Pillows,
    281–82
    Heirloom Tomato Galettes,
    43–44
    Mixed Berry Chocolate Slab Pie,
    224–26
    Puff Pastry Dough, 284–85
    Sweet Potato and Chocolate
    Squares, 158–59

Pineapple Teriyaki Sauce,
    Homemade, 292
pizza: Pizza Dough, 148–49
    Pizza with Caramelized Fennel,
    Arugula, and Lemon, 154
    Pizza with Rosemary Potatoes,
    153
plums: Stone Fruit Parfait with
    Orange-Vanilla Granola, 266
Pluots, Roasted, with Brown Sugar
    and Balsamic Vinegar, 258
Pomegranate, Gin Cocktail with
    Grapefruit and, 288
pork: Arugula with Braised Pork
    Shoulder, 132
    Summer Squash Stuffed with
    Teriyaki Pork, 164
potatoes: Creamed Swiss Chard
    in Goat Cheese on Baked
    Potatoes, 85
    Pizza with Rosemary Potatoes,
    153
    Potatoes au Gratin, 145–46
Potpie, Creamed Dill Chicken,
    with Puff Pastry, 86–87
Puff Pastry Dough, 284–85
    Creamed Dill Chicken Potpie,
    86–87
pumpkins. See also winter
    squashes
    Roasted-Pumpkin Ice Cream, 172

Quiche, Asparagus and Cippolini,
    101–3
quinoa: Cucumber Mint Quinoa
    Salad with Shallot Vinaigrette,
    203
    Roasted Parsley Root with Red
    Quinoa, 141

Radish Salsa, Spicy, 116
raspberries: Casanova Cocktail,
    230
Rhubarb-Vanilla Bread Pudding,
    109–10
rolls: Herbed Garlic Knots, 64–66
rosemary: Pizza with Rosemary
    Potatoes, 153
    Rosemary Lemonade, 74

Sabayon and Honey, Peaches with,
    269
salads: Basil Pesto Farro Salad, 71
    Chopped Kale Salad Massaged
    with Avocado, 128
    Cucumber Mint Quinoa Salad
    with Shallot Vinaigrette, 203
    Honeydew Salad with Riesling
    and Mint, 293
    Jicama Chicken Cashew Salad
    with Mustard Dressing, 157

Miso-Sesame Cucumber Salad, 204
Oro Blanco and Watercress Salad, 251
Pear-dorf Salad, 287
Picnic Pasta Salad with Roasted Tomato and Tuna, 54
Roasted-Corn Tabouli, 200
Spinach and Bacon Salad with Avocado Vinaigrette, 81
Tender Roasted Green Beans with Walnuts and Feta, 93
Vietnamese Napa Cabbage Chicken Salad, 124
Warm Kale Salad with Apples and Dried Cranberries, 127
Wilted Mizuna Mustard Salad with Shrimp, 131
Salmon, Herb-Crusted, 67
salsa: Spicy Radish Salsa, 116
Tomatillo Salsa, 215
salt, 32
sandwiches: Grilled-Zucchini Banh Mi, 178
Roasted Broccoli and Grilled Cheese Melt, 114
Smashed Cauliflower Sandwiches with Roasted Asparagus, 121
Sangria, Melon, 298
sauces: Fresh Herb Pesto, 72
Garlic Soy Dipping Sauce, 108
Homemade Barbecue Sauce from Fresh Tomatoes, 56
Homemade Pineapple Teriyaki Sauce, 292
sausage: Charred Bell Peppers and Sausage with Pearled Barley, 184
Roasted Spaghetti Squash with Sausage, 175
Scones, Roasted-Strawberry, 223
sesame: Miso-Sesame Cucumber Salad, 204
Spicy Roasted Cauliflower with Sriracha and Sesame, 118
Shallot Vinaigrette, Cucumber Mint Quinoa Salad with, 203
shishito peppers, 183
Blistered Shishito Peppers with Yuzu Kosho, 191
shrimp: Sautéed Celery and Shrimp, 94
Wilted Mizuna Mustard Salad with Shrimp, 131
Simple Syrup, 74
soups and stews: Curried Kabocha Squash and Chicken Stew, 167
Hearty Celery Root and Red Lentil Soup, 142
Summer Cream of Tomato Soup, 48

Soybean Fritters, Crispy, 97
Spaghetti, Lemon and Cream, 247
Spaghetti Squash, Roasted, with Sausage, 175
Spinach and Bacon Salad with Avocado Vinaigrette, 81
Spring Rolls, Roasted Asparagus, with Bacon, 107–8
squashes. See summer squashes; winter squashes
Sriracha and Sesame, Spicy Roasted Cauliflower with, 118
Stew, Curried Kabocha Squash and Chicken, 167
Stone Fruit Parfait with Orange-Vanilla Granola, 266
strawberries: Roasted-Strawberry Scones, 223
sugar, 32
Summer Cream of Tomato Soup, 48
summer squashes: Grilled-Zucchini Banh Mi, 178
Summer Squash Stuffed with Teriyaki Pork, 164
Zucchini-Cardamom Mini Tea Cakes, 171
sweet potatoes: Sweet Potato and Chocolate Squares, 158–59
Sweet Potato Puree, 159
sweets. See also cakes; ice cream; pies and pastries
Blackberry Cabernet Crisp with Honeyed Whipped Cream, 220–21
Brown Sugar Apricots with Vanilla Rum Ice Cream, 261–62
Chocolate Cherry Crisp, 273
Fresh Persimmon Cookies with Raisins and Nuts, 291
Marionberry Mojito Ice Pops, 233
Peaches with Sabayon and Honey, 269
Rhubarb-Vanilla Bread Pudding, 109–10
Roasted Pluots with Brown Sugar and Balsamic Vinegar, 258
Tangerine Crème Brûlée, 249–50
Swiss chard, Creamed, in Goat Cheese on Baked Potatoes, 85

Tabouli, Roasted-Corn, 200
Tacos, Habanero Chicken, 194
tangerines: Homemade Orange-Tangerine Soda, 243
Tangerine Crème Brûlée, 249–50
tarts. See also galettes
Blueberry Frangipane Tarts, 229–30
teriyaki: Homemade Pineapple

Teriyaki Sauce, 292
Summer Squash Stuffed with Teriyaki Pork, 164
Sweet Pepper and Teriyaki Chicken Skewers, 187
Tomatillo Salsa, 215
tomatoes, 41–59
Baked Eggs in Tomatoes, 51
Heirloom Tomato Galettes, 43–44
Homemade Barbecue Sauce from Fresh Tomatoes, 56
Picnic Pasta Salad with Roasted Tomato and Tuna, 54
Red Tomato Jam with Fresh Ginger, 59
Roasted Cherry Tomato and Goat Cheese Dip, 45
Summer Cream of Tomato Soup, 48
Zesty Green Tomato Pickles, 55
tools and equipment, 35
Tuna, Picnic Pasta Salad with Roasted Tomato and, 54
Turnips, Herb-Smashed, with Parmesan, 147

Vanilla Rum Ice Cream, 262
Vietnamese Napa Cabbage Chicken Salad, 124

walnuts: Pear-dorf Salad, 287
Tender Roasted Green Beans with Walnuts and Feta, 93
Watercress and Oro Blanco Salad, 251
Watermelon Mojito, 297
winter squashes: Butternut Squash Crumble, 177
Curried Kabocha Squash and Chicken Stew, 167
Roasted and Stuffed Delicata Squash Rings, 180
Roasted Gold Nugget Squash with Apples and Brown Butter, 168
Roasted Spaghetti Squash with Sausage, 175

yogurt: Stone Fruit Parfait with Orange-Vanilla Granola, 266
yuzu, 235, 255
Blistered Shishito Peppers with Yuzu Kosho, 191
Yuzu Kosho, 255

zucchini. See summer squashes

acknowledgments

It still feels like it was just yesterday when we decided to share little crumbs of our life moments on a blog. Little did we ever know or expect to be here, thinking of all the incredible folks who have connected with us over the years and who have helped us become better cooks, gardeners, and people. It would be just impossible to single out, on one page, all those who have helped influence and shape the way we understand and appreciate food. But we will never forget them and we're continually thankful for having them in our lives.

To our *blog readers* and *online friends* who have supported us over the years, we are your biggest fans. Without your daily support, encouragement, and commentary for everything that we cook, photograph, and share, we would not have written this cookbook. You all have taught us that even as strangers from across the globe, we can still be friends and participate in this worldwide family, connected through food.

Thank you to the rock-star team behind the scenes that helped us make this cookbook possible: our literary agent, *Alison Fargis* of Stonesong; our editor, *Dervla Kelly*; all *the talent at ABRAMS*; and our designer, *Amy Sly*, for nurturing this process to the beauty that it is today. Every time we turn the page, we think of your creative genius, guidance, and encouragement. Our recipes were tested in the trusted kitchens and taste buds of *Marc Shermerhorn*, *Nancy Buchanan*, *Julie Deily*, and *Alex Thomopoulos*. We could not have finished our ambitious recipe-testing process without their expertise and appetites.

Thanks to all the *authors* and *editors* who have encouraged us over the years to love our craft more every day and to inspire us to write our own cookbook.

Shawn and Sara Sedlacek, *Scott and Jaden Hair*, *Jennie Perillo*, *Jennifer Yu*, and *Elise Bauer*: Thank you for your friendship. It means the world to us.

To *our parents, siblings, and families*: We are forever grateful for your unconditional love and support. All our meals with you are cherished moments. We love you.

To *Sierra*, *Lexi*, and *our garden critters*: Thank you for making us happy, loving, laughing, and always on our toes. And to *Dante*, for being our first puppy and teaching us the meaning of unconditional love.

Finally, to *all the home cooks* out there: Continue to share your food story and make each meal with love and abandon. Each morsel you share from your kitchen is a piece of your heart and soul.